State Failure

State Failure

*The Impotence of Politics
in Industrial Society*

Martin Jänicke
Translated by Alan Braley

The Pennsylvania State
University Press

English translation © Polity Press 1990
First published in Germany as *Staatsversagen: Die Ohnmacht der Politik in der Industriegesellschaft* © R. Piper GmbH & Co. KG, München 1986

This translation first published 1990 in The United States by the Pennsylvania State University Press, Suite C, 820 North University Drive, University Park, PA 16802

Library of Congress Cataloging-in-Publication Data

Jänicke, Martin.
  [Staatsversagen. English]
  State failure: the impotence of politics in industrial society/
Martin Jänicke: translated by Alan Braley.
    p.   cm.
  Translation of: Staatsversagen. c 1986.
  Includes bibliographical references and index.
  ISBN 0-271-00714-1
  1. Economic policy. 2. Industry and state. 3. Budget deficits.
4. Social conflict. I. Title.
HD84.J3613   1990
338.9—dc20   90-36206
                                 CIP

LC 90-52798

ISBN 0-271-00714-1

Typeset in 10 on 12 pt Plantin
by Colset Pte. Ltd., Singapore
Printed in Great Britain by TJ Press, Padstow

Contents

It was clear to all that something should be done. All were agreed that we do nothing.

Politicians in the Bonn coalition, 1985

In truth, the 'power' of democratically legitimized politics is small . . . in most cases the political room for manoeuvre is getting towards vanishing point.

[Lothar Späth] Wende in die Zukunfte. Die Bundesrepublik auf dem Weg in die Informationsgesellschaft, 1985

Introduction to the English Edition

For more than a century the processes of industrialization and bureaucratization were regarded as factors of progress in society. Industrialization endowed the economy with enormous capacities, whilst bureaucratization was regarded as a form of rationalization and a means whereby policies were made more effective. Bureaucracies in the service of the democratic state and an industrialism regulated bureaucratically in this way – these were the cardinal points of the great concepts of reform during this century.

This perception overlooked three factors, however. First, processes of industrialization and bureaucratization are also processes of the accumulation of power. Second, large bureaucratic and industrial organizations often possess remarkably similar interests, working methods and internal structures; far from being natural adversaries, they are often found to be in collusion. Third, increases in the power of industry and of the state bureaucracy militate against politics and the autonomy of politics, especially when those two forms of organized power form alliances. Such alliances are particularly likely to be formed in specialized policy areas. Specialist policy networks consisting of government departments and industrial enterprises (and 'their' scientists) define the problems and the solutions outside the decisional structure of parliament, and then the structure of these networks leads with great regularity to expensive symptom-combating strategies. That is what is meant in this book by 'state failure'.

The impotence of politics in industrial society is the inability of elected politicians to take and implement decisions that run counter to the prevailing trend. Examples of such impotence are given in this book in relation to policies on health, the environment, traffic, energy, industry and finance. The illustrations are taken mainly from West Germany. Reference is also made to some other industrialized countries, though without systematic treatment of their various peculiarities. Readers in the United Kingdom should bear in mind that although generally speaking greater problems with regard to policies on the environment, the labour market and industry have arisen there than perhaps in West Germany, the state finances have developed more favourably than in many Western countries. (Large public assets have been sold, extraordinary income has arisen from North Sea oil and the savings policy has been less prudent than in almost any other Western country.) Then again, the National Health Service in the United Kingdom has different faults from the system obtaining in West Germany, in which the state largely pays the cost whilst the health services are predominantly supplied privately.

One cardinal pointer to 'state failure' is the crisis in traditional modes of state intervention. The most important evidence of this is the inability of governmental reform policies to replace the outmoded postwar pattern of industrialism, which caused a whole series of crises in energy supply, the environment, employment, state finances and other areas during the 1970s.

My research for the first edition of this book was undertaken at the height of this crisis, at the beginning of the 1980s. Since then the course of this crisis has elicited a kind of paradigm shift in the West and the East. This relates, *inter alia*, to the form which state intervention should take and is expressed in at least the beginnings of a change of direction:

- from bureaucratic centralization to decentralized solutions for problems,
- from an authoritarian style of politics to a greater emphasis on consensus,
- from short-term reactive types of policies to long-term anticipative policies,
- from bureaucratic detailed regulation to the structuring of outline conditions for the social process,
- from guidance by means of public expenditure to further guidance via public receipts (taxes, duties, scales of charges etc.)

In essence, all these tentative changes are directed at increasing the problem-solving capacity of the policy and lowering the cost of applying the solution. At the same time something akin to an economic paradigm shift is also taking place, away from 'quantitative growth' to qualitative more ecologically appropriate growth.

The English translation is based on the second, enlarged, 1990 edition of the book. It may help the understanding of structural constraints upon this change of aim, and show that new concepts should not be confused with the current change in the pattern of regulation and growth. The strong recovery that has taken place in the world economy during the 1980s should not lead to any delusions on this point. It goes without saying that the European Economic Community countries, the main objects of criticism in this book, are also benefiting from this upswing. The dynamic centre of the world economy has long since moved to Southeast Asia, however, and it is an open question whether the 'old' industrialized countries will manage to evolve a new and viable pattern of development.

In Eastern Europe we are now witnessing a revolutionary answer to the most critical form of state failure, caused by a combination of heavy industry, 'heavy bureaucracy' and authoritarian political structures. This situation seems to be quite different from that in Western industrialized countries; but this book may show that, while there are great differences in degree, pressure to change the modes of production and of state intervention is common to all industrial societies.

1 Introduction and Overview

In economic terms, state failure means supplying a country with public goods that are too highly priced and too low in quality – in both cases for structural reasons. In political terms, state failure means a chronic inability to take decisions widely agreed to be necessary – again for deepseated reasons.

Yet there is a widespread belief that the state is an all-powerful Leviathan; and indeed its powers *vis-à-vis* the citizen are constantly being extended. Incontestably, its payrolls and expenditures have been constantly on the increase. Clearly, too, its influence in the economy is increasingly felt.

There are reasons why this should be so, for in the course of industrial capitalistic development the state has shouldered an ever-increasing range of responsibilities. During the liberal competition system of the last century the state may have been able to confine its role by and large to that of a 'night watchman state', but that soon changed. In the very next stage of the development of industrial capitalism, corresponding to the long cycle of the world economy lasting from about 1895 to 1945,[1] fresh tasks were constantly devolving upon the state. As early as the end of the nineteenth century Adolph Wagner was speaking about the 'law' of increasing state expenditure.[2] This was the phase in which vigorous expansion into world markets went hand in hand with increasing centralization and 'monopolization' of industrial capital, and the banking sector began its vast expansion.

During the next long-term economic cycle, that of the post-war period, which has now come to an end, the state came to play an indispensable role. Now that the world market has been to a large extent opened up and competition is becoming increasingly fierce, the state is acquiring increasing importance both as customer and as repair centre. This development is due mainly to certain side-effects of industrial production which are adumbrated in such phrases as 'socialization of demand', 'socialization of losses' and 'external effects'.

With the buzzword of the 'market economy' the worldwide industrial system dipped into the public finances of national states – and threatened to ruin them. For the theme of this book is that, notwithstanding its growing workload and its oppressive size, the modern state is a colossus with feet of clay.

The quality of its decisions is critically defective, and the myth of its omnipotence serves to mask the extent to which its budgets are exploited by powerful distributive coalitions. Even at the cost of severe legitimatory and financial crisis, the state is constantly failing to effect urgent necessary interventions in industrial society, and policy failures are just as common within government. These restraints on intervention point to power situations and functional dependences.

This situation creates a dilemma of renewal (innovation), for the industrial structure before which the state is exhibiting its impotence is a structure that has long since passed its innovative phase and which now relies increasingly for success upon market power, and indeed on the power of its political lobbies. Countries such as West Germany have come to depend on success in selling products that have been successful during the post-war period – electricity, cars, steel, construction and chemicals. As I shall show, this orientation can be traced even in the bias of the system of taxes and subsidies. It is due to the powerful position built up over decades by various industries, and it has resulted in a sclerosis which has finally led to severe crises. Yet it creates problems in terms of both health policy and environmental policy, leading to state failure in these areas and failure to put in place a structural policy that will meet the challenge of the future.

As the superindustries grew up, so did the megabureaucracies. These compound the failures of the state in industrial society by creating the additional problem of a failure of policy within the machinery of state. Bemused by the myth of state omnipotence, politics and politicians alike have become increasingly enmeshed in the position of accepting responsibility for everything and yet deciding very little, and this casts politics very much in the role of a scapegoat. It confers an astonishing stability on the hierarchical centralized structures in industry and government, despite all the crises of unemployment, finance and ecology, for it is the politicians who carry the responsibility, even to the point of resigning if events so dictate – in return for which they enjoy high prestige whilst in office. This separation of decision from responsibility, this perfectly cocooned lack of responsibility for decisions, could in the long run become a millstone around the necks of the industrialized countries such as West Germany or the United Kingdom because formidable problems of governance and innovation are now arising. It seriously handicaps even the crisis management mechanism: crises are too seldom followed by reform and fresh initiatives. This, at least, is the danger.

This could lead to a scenario of stagnation unless the 'tank syndrome', with its tendency to gigantomania, inflexibility and externalization of problems, is adequately mastered. This is a danger threatening the industrialized countries of Eastern Europe as well, although under an entirely different set of conditions.

The alternative scenario is of a post-industrial development characterized by appropriate technologies, services, and information, having predominantly decentralized structures favouring innovation under the sign of the 'bicycle'. This is a scenario of which even present-day superindustrialism dreams, although superindustrialism may be standing in the way of its realization.

It is not yet clear which way the coin will fall. Only in the next decade will it become apparent which of these trends will prevail. Until then it seems likely that the European Economic Community (EEC) countries in particular will be wrestling with unresolved problems of unemployment and national indebtedness, which might be dubbed 'Eurosclerosis' for the reasons given above. So far, Japan and the Scandinavian countries have had more success in dealing with many aspects of these problems. These are countries with strong local communities, a penchant for long-term planning and a political culture which favours consensual processes.

Comparisons are of limited utility, and they are not to be interpreted as idealizations of particular countries. In political science they have long been used for assessing the experience of others. It is a good thing to examine such experience before developing far-reaching objectives, which otherwise would exist in a vacuum.

The comparative method does more than bring out differences, however, it also illuminates things held in common. The decisive and most problematic concern shared by all industrialized countries is their competition in world markets on terms which they themselves are mutually worsening. When states enter into economic competition with each other, they do it differently from commercial enterprises which like to keep an eye on price and quality. Nowadays industrialized states compete primarily in the form of financial aid and *laissez-faire* behaviour. Subsidies and tax waivers are compounded by non-interference. This strategy might confer some economic advantage if it were pursued by only a few countries (say the underdeveloped ones). But if everybody competes in this way against everybody else, costs rise for everybody – the cost of 'export promotion', the cost of the competitive disadvantages which such promotion fails to eliminate, and the manifold costs of the still unsolved problems unleashed by unregulatable industrialism, from destruction of the environment to unemployment.

The title of this book needs some clarification. 'State failure', 'ungovernability', 'institutional sclerosis' are epithets readily used by the conservatives and neo-liberals in politics.[3] On this view the greatest failure of the state is seen in the 'inflation of expectations' of its citizens, whose increased mobilization makes them less amenable to governance. Trade unions and other associations, in concert with competing political parties and their election pledges, also help to drive the state into impotence or debt, and in this way 'state failure' becomes a war-cry against the welfare state and its beneficiaries. This usually leads to a call for stronger leadership, to protect market forces against what are seen as the irrational results of democratic decision-making processes. This criticism of the state has a long tradition; in Germany it goes back at least to criticism of the Weimar Republic by the authoritarian lawyer Carl Schmitt.[4] Nowadays it has almost become official political doctrine in the Anglo-Saxon countries.

There are reasons for the criticism, which we shall discuss below. But the concept of state failure just mentioned does more to mask these causes than to expose them, given the existing positions of strength and vested interests. Therefore I am more interested in what lies behind this understanding. If we turn the picture round from ungovernable citizens with their greedy desires, we shall find something that merits close study.

I published several works on this subject at the end of the 1970s, and I now take up and develop those themes, especially the arguments I advanced in the book *Wie das Industriesystem von seinen Misständen profitiert* (How the industrial system profits from its abuses) published in 1979.[5]

That book dealt with the increasing susceptibility of the industrial structure of a country such as West Germany to develop problems. I showed how environmental, health, education or even internal security problems were being increasingly paid for via the state. My contention was that the structure of industrial supply increasingly necessitated expensive remedial and damage-repair projects. This situation resulted from failure by politicians to take preventive action.

As a result of that research I predicted that this course on which super-industry was embarked could be neither legitimized nor financed in the long run – a judgement vindicated by subsequent events, for since then ecological parties have made an issue of it and public debt has reached crisis proportions.

In the meantime there has been an upsurge of enthusiasm for renewal. Protection of the environment, more appropriate technologies, a greater emphasis on post-industrial developments have been taken up by a whole movement of writers on politics.[6] Renewal is everywhere in vogue. Those who see in this the harbinger of permanent recovery should examine the task really facing an innovative thrust sufficient to overcome the crisis.

This time my most important source was not the University library; I relied mainly on a kind of 'research by doing'. I collected experiences (a) at central government level, in the Planning Department of the Federal Chancellery at Bonn, (b) at provincial parliament level, in the Chamber of Deputies at Berlin, and (c) at the grass-roots level of politics in a number of citizens' initiatives and parties. However, in addition to these specific experiences I also (d) constantly kept abreast of the self-revealing utterances and statistics emanating from politicians, businessmen and economists in the industrialized countries. Hence this book is not offered as a contribution to the specialist literature on political science. Many important authors are not quoted here, simply because the subject is so vast as to call for innumerable literature references.

The work is intended for those engaged in and observing the political arena who are looking for explanations of developments that are obviously undesirable, and who will not be fobbed off with superficial naive proposals for bringing about change.

2 The Role of the State in the Industrial System

What is the industrial system?

The industrial system is an invention of capitalism, and it still exerts its greatest effects, whether for creation or destruction, wherever profit is the overriding motive for investment.[1] Profit implies growth, and growth is the determinative characteristic of the industrial system. However, the industrial system is not confined to capitalism and its growth is not solely due to profit-seeking business. It is true that socialist countries in the Soviet mould have revolutionized the power relationships and property structures of capitalism. But the objective of catching up with the capitalistic prototype of the industrial system and overtaking it has led not only to ever-increasing reliance upon the economy and technology of the West but also, and above all, to an ever-broadening involvement in the world market of capitalism. And these countries, newcomers to the world market, behave just like capitalist corporations in a competitive environment. Moreover, this affects their internal structure as well. It is true that the planning structure within the Council for Mutual Economic Assistance (CMEA) countries allows them to set up forward-looking structural policies and controls of technology, but they have so far made little use of these facilities. They have neither developed problem-free alternative technologies nor created alternatives to centrally directed large-scale highly specialized industry. Indeed, there has been less opposition in those countries to the gigantomania of big industry than under capitalism, although they too suffer from similar problems and a continuous increase in social costs.[2]

Thus the industrial system, although a product of capitalism, has spread throughout the world. Nevertheless, I do not subscribe to the theory of a unified industrial society. It makes a tremendous difference whether a system typically suffers from a permanent capital surplus or a chronic shortage of capital. It *does* matter whether the banks or the party bureaucracy dominate the process of industrial decision-making. Equally important are the means of social protest afforded by the political system (because these increase the society's potential for innovation). Nor is the part played by private consumption in a system irrelevant, or whether or not private waste is a condition of growth. This is explained in greater detail later, so I shall confine myself here to a broad description of the capitalist industrial system that is governed by a 'Western'-type parliamentary bureaucracy.

Industry is both a structure and a dynamic principle. Its structural characteristics are specialization, centralization and rationalization. This structure – the mass production of particular goods by large industrial concerns based on the currently most favourable ratio between expenditure and revenue – is dynamic in several respects.

- Mass production favours a constant expansion of markets.
- The ratio of expenditure to revenue can be constantly improved through technology.
- The 'technical progress' thereby engendered creates fresh demand.
- The capital accumulation involved in all this entails centralization.[3]

A special feature of the dynamism of industrialism is its bias towards external and internal totalization:

- externally through the creation of global markets (internationalization);
- internally through the universalization of industrial principles – it penetrates more and more areas of society and aspects of living (though this gives rise to an increasing dependence on services, with the real possibility that the 'tertiary sector' may develop a dynamism of its own, independent of the industrial sector).

The creation of problems and their externalization through passing them on to others is a further aspect of the dynamics of industry, and arguably the most important one.

The rationality of industry is operating efficiency. An individual firm may have multinational dimensions, but its costing procedures exclude considerations extraneous to the firm, in so far as they are cost factors and not political impositions. This built-in disregard of common interests in the profitability calculations of individual companies (in Comecon as well) is a universal characteristic, and it is reinforced by processes which divorce cause (a production decision) from effect (the external damage). Above all, it is *forced* upon companies by competition, if the costs of socially palliative measures entail competitive disadvantages.

Functional definition of the state

The industrial system does not have a centre. Since it disregards the overall social preconditions and consequences of its exploitation of capital, labour and technology by individual enterprise, the state is constantly acquiring new functions in this regard.

THE REGULATORY FUNCTION

With the growth of specialization the interdependence of the various economic agents and the complexity of their relationships grow. This leads to an increasing demand for regulation and legislation by the state. Without this increasing regulatory activity the predictability of economic activity, and hence its effectiveness, would be radically diminished.

THE LEGITIMATION FUNCTION

The second function of the state concerns legitimation. This is a task not for the machinery of the state but for the custodians of the national will, in other words the persons and institutions in parliament and government who have the power of decision. These 'decision-makers' decide very little, but they carry the responsibility for nearly everything. It is politicians who have to bear the responsibility for unemployment and to justify it, even though it was private enterprise that made the wrong investment decisions. It is 'politicians' who have to take responsibility for the failure of 'their' bureaucracy and defend it, although they are scarcely in a position to evaluate the details of such a complex organization and, unlike career civil servants, have only a brief tenure. When controllers and 'decision-makers' do no more than rubber-stamp decisions taken by others, so that the political function of crystallizing the national will degenerates into a process of legitimation, politics becomes increasingly a scapegoat function. This is perhaps the major dilemma of our constitutional institutions, and more will be said about it in subsequent chapters.

THE INFRASTRUCTURE FUNCTION

Specialized mass production has some general prerequisites which it is difficult to integrate into corporate growth costings. One of these prior needs is the creation of a pool of adequately skilled workers, and this is better entrusted to the 'community' or to the educational policy of the state. This policy, like policy on research, then becomes increasingly important in the process of industrial development. Other examples are public highways and, in general, the provision of all those infrastructure facilities that are essential to the conduct of business.

THE NUISANCE ABATEMENT FUNCTION

Even more important are the overall consequences of production – the ill effects which industrial production by individual enterprises has on the social and physical environment. Pollution of the air and water, the problems of waste disposal and noise pollution are some of these effects known to economists as externalities. So are the consequences of a sickness profile largely determined by industrial conditions, with which the state has to deal. The increasing differences in wealth between different regions or sectors of the economy, as for example between industry and agriculture, which are constantly imposing fresh strains on the state's capacity for redistribution, are also among the overall results of production. And of course the specialized 'economic agents' leave to the community the task of finding new jobs for workers who are regularly being displaced by increased labour productivity. The same is true of that growing segment of the older population that is compelled to accept ever earlier retirement from the production process. Then there are the indirect consequences of an increasing level of industrialization – urbanization, crime resulting from frustration, alienation, excessive demands on adaptability, and a constantly rising skill demand threshold which only some members of society can satisfy.

The two most important economic functions of the state are the services it renders in advance of and subsequent to the production process, namely the infrastructure and the nuisance abatement functions. It is largely these functions which create the enormous financial requirements, which the state then lobs back into the court of 'economic growth'. This growth motivation is behind the propensity of government to create optimum production conditions for industry and to minimize its burden of costs. Thus the state becomes an engine of growth *sui generis* in the industrial system and from this point of view it is dependent upon the industrial system.[4]

The points mentioned so far relate to the functional interdependence between the state and the industrial system with its interest in growth. These functional relationships are important – more important than personal relationships, 'tie-ups', career moves from government to industry and vice versa – because they show that power dependence and corruption are by no means the only reasons why government decisions are to a large extent biased in favour of the interests of industry. The widely held view that all would be well if industry were democratized or if the right people were employed in government service – that business would then be oriented towards the common good – disregards the logic of the functional relationship between the industrial system and the state. Nonetheless, no observer of the political scene would deny that political power play is responsible for influences and pressures not attributable to this functional interdependence as such. These power situations are the reverse side of the dependence of the state on the industrial system.

The role of politics in the power structure of industrial societies

If 'power' is a central theme of political science, then 'social power' is also part of the syllabus. The idea that power is the province of the state alone is fostered by considering only absolute and authoritarian states. Applied to the constitutional states of the West it is a figment of an idealized simplistic world view (see the appendix, p. 138ff). It follows that a comparative study of the power structures of a country must include not only data on the state and its constitution but also

- the structures of business and its 'constitution',
- the structures of the interest organizations and their 'constitution' and
- the structures of the media and their 'constitution'.

One of the most significant distinctions between the political power of the state and social and economic power is that the power of the state is institutionalized whereas social power usually is not. This corresponds to Max Weber's distinction between power and authority. 'By *power* is meant that opportunity existing within a social relationship which permits one to carry out one's own will even against resistance and regardless of the basis on which the opportunity rests. By *authority* is meant the opportunity to have a command of a given specified content obeyed by a given group of persons.'[5] Thus authority is power institutionalized, ordered and legitimated. It is confined to specific persons and to commands with a specific content, whereas power, according to Max Weber, is 'sociologically amorphous'. It is not subject to any need for legitimation or to any institutional rules. It might well be contended that the very lack of these constraints favours the power of society over the state and its institutionalized authority. The same is true of the principle of public dealings in a parliamentary system. Such institutional restrictions repose only on the will-forming institutions of the state, but not on the private oligarchies.

But the problem of state power is even more complicated, for it also consists of the internal, relationship of state power to the bureaucracy. It is only the institutionalized 'decision-makers' – the politicians – who experience the need for legitimation. The bureaucracy, in contrast, is shielded by its 'masters' with regard to legitimation. Hence when speaking about the state we must always distinguish clearly between the will-forming institutions of parliament and government and the state bureaucracy.

The problem of state failure and the ungovernability of the power of society in the industrial system begins with the bureaucracy and with political failure resulting from the weak position of the decision-makers and controllers against the executive. Not without reason do we affirm that the 'decision-makers', right up to the head of government, have a primarily legitimatory function for the machinery of state (this is why an actor can be a perfectly appropriate occupant of the President's office). This does not prevent the formal will-forming institutions from *also* taking decisions, especially when stalemate occurs within the bureaucracy or conflicts arise between the interests of bureaucrats and industrialists. By 'decisions' we do not mean simply ratifications of the ordinary processes of reaching an accommodation. Decisions taken from political foresight or to prevent a crisis would rather be directed against the normal course of events, and in this sense those persons and bodies constitutionally charged with crystallizing and formulating the will of the nation, and enforcing it, are in an equivocal position.

These considerations explain why the power of the bureaucracy is here accorded first place among the factors of social power confronting politics as an institutionalized process of decision-making.

The power of the bureaucracy

Just as industrialization seems to have entered a late crisis-ridden phase, so also does the process of bureaucratization which is closely connected with it. In the tradition of Max Weber the process of bureaucratization is regarded as a historically unavoidable necessity. But from today's perspective the question increasingly arises how much this process owed to the logic of the facts and to what extent it was conditioned by the logic of power.

Bureaucracy is omnipresent in politics for somewhat the same reasons as industry is omnipresent in the economy. Specialization, centralization, rationalization, routinization and the permanent career structure give both these forms of organization their advantage over more decentralized simpler forms of politics and economy. However, it is not only their efficiency that enables these centralized and specialized megabureaucracies to prevail in this way and to displace smaller forms of organization that are still of manageable size. Bureaucratic and industrial forms of organization also have the advantage in terms of power. Consequently their victorious advance in politics and the economy is by no means solely attributable to 'objective' causes.[6]

The logic of the facts in this process might be that each fresh stage of institutionalized crisis management gives rise to an increase in bureaucracy. Such an increase would then be a side-effect of political development in the sense adumbrated further on (see chapter 9 and the appendix). This may be true in large measure.

Yet in two respects this objective logic of the development of bureaucracy must be called into question. For one thing, there is no iron law which says that the social process must develop in such a way as to produce a large number of problems calling for bureaucratic solutions. Then again, it is questionable to what extent the bureaucratic method of responding to problems can be regarded as appropriate. An increasing proportion of the social problems arising in the industrial system stems from interdependence and complex concatenations of effects, which a centralized departmentalized bureaucracy is particularly unfitted to perceive (see p. 37ff).

The trend of costs shows how ill adapted is the process of bureaucratization nowadays to the objective logic of an industrial society. A system-functional bureaucracy would be a cheap bureaucracy, and yet one of the reasons for the escalation of the cost of government is the internal consumption of the bureaucracy itself. If income privileges are taken as an index of the power position of groups, then the power of the bureaucracy is impressively illustrated by the increase in the upper income groups in the public service. Even during the economy drive undertaken between 1980 and 1983 the Bonn bureaucracy increased its proportion of the top two salary brackets (the savings were made in the lower echelons).[7]

This process indicates more than just the favoured position of the bureaucracy in the salary shareout. It also points to the constantly increasing cost of hierarchical centralism in the state. The expensive high income groups are those of the central bureaucracy. Local government is distinctly more economical for the taxpayer. As I shall show, this applies most of all to its management of public finances.

So the problem of bureaucracy is about the upper levels and the sizes of administrations. This could be illustrated from the federal states both of West Germany and the United States. It is particularly marked in the EEC. The myth of the machinery of state as an *instrument* (see the appendix) is exposed almost of itself in these cases. The political echelon of the decision-makers nearly always fails with regard to the bureaucracy in two ways: as an imaginary overall bureaucrat and as an overall capitalist. In the former case bureaucratic special interests pose an increasing threat to the overall financing, and in the latter case these costs are a drag on the macroeconomy, especially when the benefit is small. The problem of the controllability of the machinery of state is treated in greater detail later (see p. 22ff). This is not only a problem of the span of control of subordinates – the number of civil servants has increased enormously – it is also the dilemma of project monitoring that has run out of control, for the special matters requiring political solutions have multiplied exponentially.

However, the number of ministers and members of parliament – the 'politicians' in the narrower sense of the scapegoat roles to be handed out – has not changed. A policy that not only invoked technical innovation but also paid attention to the needful prerequisites in the field of social innovation would have to make fundamental changes here. It will not suffice merely to multiply efforts aimed at political control at the centre. The change must involve making the whole of the machine more manageable; and this can be achieved only by decentralization.

At all events, there is no secret about the problem. We have only to compare the number of civil servants that a minister in the nineteenth century had under his control with the complement of a modern bureaucracy. Yet the demands on political control by the minister have remained unchanged, although their functions have certainly been reversed. That a minister must nowadays be prepared to resign because he did not forestall some failure of the bureaucrats emphasizes the role of politics as an instrument of the bureaucracy. We all know the tale of the 'luckless' politician who tries to do his own thing in 'his ministry', who really regards decision and control as something for which he is responsible; and the tale of the realist and 'doer' who vigorously promotes his departmental head's brief in external dealings and has 'his people' behind him – because he is 'their man'. In the light of all these privileges, unavoidable freedom from control and, above all, specialist knowledge there is every reason to surmise that, since the politicians still have the responsibility for decisions, the power of the administrations to define the problems and solutions is very great. However, the way in which problems are defined determines the response strategies, and the response strategies are just as much coloured by interest as are the bureaucracies themselves.[8]

The neutrality of interest (or simple obedience to the decision-maker) is seen most clearly to be restricted if we consider the bureaucracy and its clientele. Every bureaucracy is surrounded by favoured clients who, like the bureaucracy, benefit from current budgetary dispositions. In the case of social security these may be old age pensioners or persons in receipt of social assistance of one kind or another. But more usually they are companies and trading organizations. This is true of the building administrations and the construction lobby, and of other important departments and the organized interests competing for a share of their budgets. In their cases it is the closely interwoven functional interests of the departmental bureaucracies and the industrial sectors that constitute a formidable counterweight to the nominal decision-makers of the state.

Bureaucracy–industry complexes

Thus close coalitions between civil servants and industrialists in areas of state activity are especially apt to limit the independence of political decision-makers. An important element in the power of the industrial system is the specialization of industrial interest complexes, whereby particular growth interests can be brought to bear which do not coincide with the general interest in growth. We have of course particularly in mind those specialized industries which depend to a greater or lesser extent on government orders. The state as customer – as 'public demand' – has grown in importance as industry has developed and the 'state proportion' (the percentage of gross national product (GNP) represented by public expenditure) has risen in proportion. There are many reasons for this. In the first place it reflects the growing role of the state as a crisis manager and promoter of growth. But the 'public' market also expands as the state assumes more and more tasks which are themselves largely a condition or consequence of the growth of large-scale industry. From the industry point of view the attractiveness of the state as a buyer, despite protestations of belief in the market economy, is obvious.

Even in the era of the absolute monarchies the most coveted position was that of 'supplier to the Court'. It enhanced the supplier's status, if nothing else. The cachet is not so important nowadays – but the financial advantages are considerable.

To begin with, because of medium-term financial planning government requirements are far more predictable than private demand. Then again, civil servants are as a rule much less tight-fisted with the taxpayer's money than are private customers with their own, if only because the departmental budget is likely to be curtailed if they do not spend it all, and it is easy for competitors to agree upon a price-fixing arrangement when dealing with a single customer. The specialist industrial supplier is in any event closer to his particular bureaucracy-customer than the taxpayer, who seldom obtains access to the administration. The specialist industrial supplier is in most cases the only important interlocutor with whom a civil servant in charge of a sectional budget is dealing; he is most obliging, full of useful ideas and information, and frequently has good contacts with 'the politicians' and the media.[9]

Industries which specialize largely in facets of state activity and depend upon the relevant budgets form functional interrelationships with their opposite numbers in the bureaucracy. These I term 'bureaucracy–industry complexes'.[10]

The military–industrial complex is the oldest and best known of these. Apart from the private trade in arms, it lives solely on government orders. This is also very largely true of the construction industry complex which, owing to its many links with other branches of industry, has hitherto been the favourite lever for promotion of growth by governments. The agrobusiness complex also draws a considerable proportion of its income from state budgets in the form of subsidies. The powerful medical–industrial complex is financed almost preponderantly by public or government-organized funding. Then there is a complex about which nothing is published, yet which absorbs very considerable amounts of public money. I would call it the financial complex, both public and private. Basically it refers to that part of the banking sector which lives by selling credit to the state, and hence works closely with government finance departments. Lastly, the scientific complex (big science) has the state as one of its most important customers.

The list also extends to the eco-industry complex which produces the good of a 'better environment', the security complex which produces the good of 'internal security' and the energy supply complex, which offers reliable supplies of energy in superabundance. The last-named (especially coal and nuclear power) is a voracious consumer of subsidies, and it also benefits to an unusual extent from state regulations and privileges, including a monopoly on the sale of electricity.

At first sight the 'road traffic complex' appears to be relatively independent of the state, but it depends for its growth on road building by the state, and when we come to examine state finances we shall find that it enjoys other state preferences of no mean order.

Thus special coalitions of interests between the bureaucracy and private industry have come into existence far below the levels at which governmental objectives are defined. Both for the public and for the political decision-makers these are also coalitions which have considerable powers of definition. Therefore the coalitions have a large influence in formulating the technocratic strategies of the state, a circumstance which explains why so many government objectives are formulated as production objectives.

This trend leads in the end to a depoliticization of state activity, about which Gerd Winter has the following to say: 'The motivation of specific behaviour by means of orders, prohibitions and permits is replaced by the channelling of money flows according to technical criteria, and this virtually uses the political structures designed for control as handholds with which to surmount them, so to speak.'[11]

The power of industry

The problem of industrial power is evident from considerations of size alone. Large multinational corporations such as General Motors, Shell and the like each have worldwide turnovers in excess of the budget of Australia, and an economic output greater than that of some industrialized states.

To the political decision-makers, industrial power presents itself above all as the power of refusal, in line with the functional importance of industry to the state. As elsewhere, industrial power finds expression quite inconspicuously as freedom of decision under the conditions of competition: industry invests preferentially in locations where its own requirements are met. Large-scale unemployment is another argument underpinning a power position of this type for capitalist industry. Besides strengthening the hold of the corporation on its own employees, it strengthens its hand in discussions with government. All sorts of demands can be strongly reinforced by playing the employment card.

The very fact that the individual firm acts as an interest-promoting organization, however, engenders industrial power. It is the interest of a producer seeking to further its ends on a full-time professional career basis and deploying its considerable financial and organizational power.

This is reinforced by the solidarity of business interests, especially those having a supplier – customer relationship or interlocking capital structures; there is also the solidarity of producers as a whole, convinced that setbacks for one business sector are likely to have unfavourable repercussions throughout the business community.

Furthermore, the banking system has the effect of focusing the power of industry, an effect at least equal to that of the pervasive growth-orientation. In West Germany, and also elsewhere, banks hold a position of strength in the economy over and above their function as dispensers of credit, through their direct or indirect shareholdings in industry. In West Germany they are also represented on the supervisory boards of the vast majority of joint stock companies, and the power of three large banks (Deutsche Bank, Dresdner Bank and Commerzbank) is especially noteworthy. This 'finance capital' role, observed by Hilferding some 80 years ago,[12] has acquired immense significance. It strengthens the influence of outsiders in the corporate decisions of individual companies whilst increasing the centralization of power and decision-making affecting industry as a whole.

But the trade unions too can usually be relied on for support in championing the interests of individual companies in their dealings with the state. Of course, trade unions are primarily in the business of defending existing jobs in their particular sectors of production. To the extent that they develop into specialized oligarchic wage-raising machines they will share the interest of the sector as a whole in profits and growth. This explains why works councils will support orders for arms manufacture or processes detrimental to the environment in their companies. (In contrast, trade unions taking part in more wide-ranging cooperative processes and alive to the overall needs of the economy can play an important part in redirecting corporate aims and in changing structures in a socially beneficial direction. This is true in many respects of the Scandinavian countries and Austria.)

Another advantage enjoyed by industry in its relations with the state derives from its technological monopoly combined with the freedom to make its own investment decisions. This automatically puts the state at a disadvantage when it contemplates precautionary intervention, for the state usually takes action only after economic *faits accomplis*, such as the creation of investment and jobs. Thus if the state considers the probable consequences so harmful that prohibitory measures are justified, this amounts to substantial economic damage to the company concerned, which runs counter to the short-term growth interests of the government itself.

Furthermore, in many conflicts with the public interest as formulated by the state, industry can count upon a virtual ally: the consumer. The seductive argument runs as follows: should not problems connected with road use, energy production, tobacco consumption, alcoholism or the cretinization of the masses by the new media be overcome by 'changing consumer behaviour'? Clearly, industrial capitalism is skilled at manipulating democratic formulae. It is preeminently skilled at discovering human weaknesses; and with alienation, meaninglessness and, in Marcuse's term, 'one-dimensionality' in industrial society, these weaknesses are increasing.[13] That is what makes stupefaciants such as alcohol or television, and the sense of power induced by driving high-powered cars, so appealing. Moreover, a whole range of products, from noise-reducing double glazing to sleeping tablets, is consumed from necessity rather than choice.

Nevertheless there is no denying that the practical usefulness of many goods is what causes consumers to abet their production. For most people, using less energy or driving fewer kilometres would be a real sacrifice, though surveys have shown that most would be willing to make such a sacrifice. Experiments in West Germany with car-free Sundays have led to the same conclusion – provided that the sacrifice is not confined to a few idealists. It must therefore be made compulsory after public discussion or by official promulgation if it is to be effective. Since in most cases it proves impossible to organize sufficient pressure at the grass-roots level, the buck is passed to 'consumer behaviour', to which producers can then appeal as justification.

The power of the media

In all the capitalist industrial countries, the press depends on advertising placed by private industry for more than half of its revenue. In many Western countries such as the United States, Canada, Japan and Italy, this applies to radio and television as well. We are talking about business enterprises which have the normal interests of such organizations, from bank loans to collective agreements – enterprises which in many cases are themselves owned by businesses, and which share the general business outlook inasmuch as advertising revenue rises when the economy is flourishing. Like other branches of business, they try to achieve monopolies.

But even the structure of the radio broadcasting companies under public law in West Germany, now being challenged by a commercialization of broadcasting, gives profit-oriented business interests in combination with conservative organizations a strong position.

Similarly in international news broadcasting the dominant position held by a few privately owned Western agencies results in a biased situation.

The fact that during recent times the media have paid attention to the neglected public interest at least in the form of warnings about unsavoury situations has to do not only with the nature of those problems but also with the specific 'market situation' of privately owned publicity organs. Without doubt this market is also conditioned by the anxiety of citizens about the future and their concern about the way in which industry is damaging the quality of life. Therefore some of these concerns are voiced – but often in strident terms and in ways more likely to increase the perplexity of those affected.

The power of industrial organization

Not only are industrial enterprises in themselves huge interest organizations; industry is further strongly represented in the organizational structure of developed societies. Directly or indirectly, industrial interests are dominant in their organizational structure. The 'power of organized interests' recognized by Eschenburg[14] at an earlier stage is above all the power of industrial interest groups. Furthermore, as Olson and Offe emphasized more than two decades ago, the prevailing organizational structure is determined by the dominant business interests.[15]

On the one hand, there are the strongly organized business and growth interests and, on the other hand, the more or less weakly organized interests outside the orbit of business and industry – the interests of pensioners, children, housewives, tenants, the unemployed, the sick, recipients of social assistance, students, all of whom are consumers of the good and bad effects of the industrial system. Common interests, such as the interest in peace or in future quality of life, are organized outside the business–industrial sector and are therefore inadequately organized.

The imbalance between the interests of business–industry and those of the rest of the population as regards the level of organization stands out starkly if we contemplate the time budget of the entire population of an industrial society. Assuming that every citizen of a country has interests during every hour of his life, from his interest in work to his interest in sleeping at night, then the annual time of the whole population can be a measure of the effectiveness of the system of associations in looking after public interests.

The whole population of West Germany does not even spend 8 per cent of its time at work. As working hours are reduced, as life expectancy increases and as more time is spent in education and training or even on the unemployment register, so this annual quota of time not spent in gainful employment tends to grow. In any event, only a minority of the population is employed, and the working time of those who *are* in employment amounts to only about one-fifth of their annual time budget. This accounts for the low ratio of working time to total time of the population (figure 1).

What becomes of the rest of the time and the life interests that occupy it, to say nothing of the interests of future generations, which are very inadequately represented even in the employment sector? In this respect there exist such

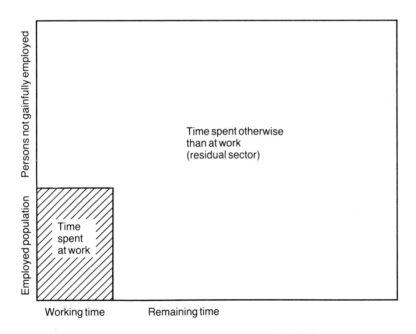

Figure 1   Annual time budget of the total population of West Germany.

structural barriers as to merit description of organizationally underprivileged interests in the residual sector. In French social criticism (Gorz, Touraine) this inequality of organizational power is actually regarded as a new class struggle situation.

Following Offe[16] we can set out this organizational inequality in tabular form. Table 1 is not intended to minimize the many and varied conflicts that arise within the employment sector, notably between capital and labour. Its real subject is the additional line of conflict that is of special importance to the formation of the alternative movement or post-materialistic opposition.

The nation state in the era of internationalization

From the standpoint of the nation state or its regions or local government areas, industrial power also poses problems because it is international. This applies to the world market and the superindustries operating in it (about which more will be said later). By the same token it applies to the now largely uncontrollable flows of international finance and the banking system which has become globally autonomous. It applies to the internationally unified news industry and the small number of agencies comprising it.

But the industrialized countries also have another problem: the loss of sovereignty caused by economic and military blocs. It is my contention that the ways in which blocs are formed inhibit the potential for independent creative problem-solving strategies in Europe. It is taken for granted in the West that this is true of the Eastern bloc countries. But how do things look in our own camp?

The EEC has been taking powers of decision away from member countries in favour of a decisional structure that is subject to very little democratic scrutiny but is developing a strong bureaucratic centralism which is becoming a natural associate of the multinationals in Europe. 'Eurosclerosis' has much to do with the fact that this bureaucracy has provided the whole structural conservatism of multinationally concentrated industrial power with a relatively undisturbed and highly subsidized field of operations.

Decisions of the EC Council of Ministers are also binding upon national parliaments. What an astonishing breach of democratic constitutional principles! And these decisions often set lower standards than those that are deemed to call for regulation in some EC countries. In environmental protection matters, for example, the EC's tendency to 'harmonize' requirements at a low level and the incentives for innovation display the same minimalism.

Probably it is the military blocs that place the greatest constraint upon the

Table 1   The unequal organizational power of interests in the employment and the residual sector

	Employment sector	Residual sector
Role in society	Production Subject of the social process Growth interests	Consumption Object of the social process Protection interests
Share of annual time budget of the whole population	< 10% Falling	> 90% Rising
Signs of unequal organizational power	High degree of organization High functional importance to the social process (consequences of refusal) Highly centralized Highly specialized Full-time (career) promotion of interests Competent promotion of interests Regulated (institutionalized) conflict resolution Large financial resources Strong parliamentary representation	low degree of organization Low functional importance to the social process Marginalized Very diffuse Sideline (part-time) promotion of interests Amateurish promotion of interests Unregulated conflict resolution Small financial resources Weak parliamentary representation

freedom of action of individual states. This is quite obvious in respect of the subservient role of Europeans in relation to the 'leading power' in their respective blocs. In this matter, however, the problem of the sovereignty of individual states resides not only in the leadership role played by the military–industrial complex of the superpower in question but also in the association between the military sectors of the allied countries, which gives them tremendous powers of definition and persuasion *vis-à-vis* their own governments.

The extent to which the object of the organization, namely national and international security, is transmuted into nothing more than an arena for bestowing respectability on a congeries of vested interests is clear from the decision taken by the North Atlantic Treaty Organization (NATO) that defence budgets are to be increased by 3 per cent annually in real terms. If state failure be regarded above all as a mismatch between the price and quality of public goods, then this mismatch is increased by the international dimension. NATO countries pay on average an appreciably higher proportion of their GNP for security than do countries which are not NATO members,[17] some of which might be regarded as under greater threat because of their geographical propinquity to the adversary. One thinks of Finland, Austria or Japan. In the light of the military activities of the bloc-leader, the United States, in the Mediterranean or the Gulf, it is difficult to see that this disproportionately high burden of expenditure on armaments results in greater security.

The impotence of parliaments

Parliaments cannot be stronger than the state as a whole, though they may easily be weaker. This, in fact, is our main problem at the present time.

It is a long-standing complaint that parliaments in most Western countries have undergone *de facto* institutional debilitation and that they do no more than ratify decisions taken elsewhere.[18] This complaint has seldom been seriously contested with supporting factual evidence; my own parliamentary experience, at least, has confirmed it. In 1981 as a member of the Berlin Chamber of Deputies I was able to study a parliament in a relatively strong position. For two years the Weiszäcker government had been a minority government. Moreover the party granting it support, the Free Democratic Party (FDP), was split and it was difficult to estimate the number of dissidents. Yet during those two years there was only one occasion on which the majority of this government was in danger, and the occasion was an increase in the tax on dogs, for which the 'regulation' voting had not been organized in good time. The situation did not become clear until the division was called.

It is impossible to overestimate the extent to which administrations get their way, either alone or with their organized clients. Even a cursory glance will reveal an abundance of reasons for the weak position of parliament *vis-à-vis* the bureaucracy. For instance, administrations dissimulate the knowledge available to them behind a welter of information. This modern form of the disclosed state secret (Poulantzas) creates a massive amount of work. The critical deputy (or journalist) will have to weary his eyes with reading if he wants to keep track of the administration's activities. All too often he eventually realizes that he is no better informed than he was originally. If the deputy gives up this hare-and-tortoise chase and starts an initiative of his own, he seldom has the parliamentary pull to counteract the bureaucratic veto ('not feasible in law', 'not within our remit', 'not feasible in the present budgetary situation' etc.)

The parliamentary day is commonly taken up by innumerable special subjects dealt with in working parties of one or two deputies, and the rest of the group perforce relies upon their judgement in the matter.[19] These few group specialists are of course particularly exposed to influence from persons or groups with special interests, from glossy specialist information services to other attentions.

Many reasons could be adduced for the impotence of parliamentary politics 'in the state', but there is no need to go into them when more far-reaching criticisms are on the agenda. For the question is no longer whether and to what extent parliamentary politics are in a position to instrumentalize the government machine. The new quality of the development is shown in the contrary assumption, that the government machine is in a position to instrumentalize the institutions of parliament and, with them, the party state itself. Thus Poulantzas, following Agnoli and others, characterizes the parties participating in the parliamentary 'changing of the guard' as 'transmission belts for decisions of the executive': 'Parties nowadays have almost ceased to be even a locus of political formulation and the elaboration of compromises and alliances based on more or less clearly defined programmes . . . they are being transformed into mere channels for popularizing and propagating policies of the state, which for the most part are decided upon outside the parties.[20]

Let the reader be the judge of the validity of this contention. It is at least apparent that the would-be governing parties give priority to the task of competitively promoting powerful special interests and decisions, and that in this process the 'objective arguments' of the government machine figure prominently.

The 'assimilation' of the established parties, already perceived by Luhmann in 1969, would be explained in so far as the thesis of the instrumentalization of politics by the government machine proved to be correct. Luhmann attributes the fact that 'the result of the election makes virtually no difference' to the fact that the parties are in competition for the same objective, namely to gain positions in government.[21] Another explanation would be that the associations of organized business interests are sufficiently well represented in all the established parties and thus win every election. A third explanation is the explanation that has already been advanced, namely that the constricting power, finance and functional situations of the state are only reflected in parliament and the party system, and this in turn places special constraints upon parliamentary politics in the state.

These explanations are not mutually exclusive. Anybody aiming at securing 'governmental responsibility' knows that he must first of all accept responsibility for the activities of the government machine. He also knows – or will soon learn – that he will have to explain the 'objective constraints' of the state out in the provinces. Consequently it is not realistic to arouse too many expectations in the electorate which in view of the role of government 'would be unrealizable'. By the same token it is hardly possible to adopt after a change of government more radical policies, completely different from those inherent in 'responsible government'.

It follows that an instrumentalization of parliament and the multi-party system hinges upon the governmental role either practised or aimed at by a party. Nonetheless, the questions whether, to what extent, how and why politicians use the administration or vice versa calls for discussion in greater depth.

The scapegoat role of politics

Politics and administration are two different things. Nobody can doubt this since Max Weber wrote about it. Politicians are by definition mandated to govern, a function which is defined by such important tasks as planning, decision-making, control and coordination. Their opposite numbers are the various echelons of civil servants. The general understanding is that the latter have executive or executant functions. Their activity is justified and legitimated by the fact that they carry out the will of democratically appointed politicians and are subject to their control. To that extent, it is only logical that the elected politicians should also carry the responsibility for the activity of the machinery of state.

That, then, is the formal situation. If it is to have substance, politicians governing by virtue of a parliamentary majority must answer for mistakes made by the administration as if they were their own. If, however, the title is only a fiction as described in the myth of instrumentality (see the appendix, p. 140) parliamentary politics have only a legitimating function. In this case we have a division between those who decide and implement and those who carry the responsibility for this process and justify it. This division is the crucial problem of contemporary parliamentary politics.

This separation between decision and responsibility is so momentous because it characterizes both politics 'within the state' and the policy 'of the state'. By its whole status in law, business and industry as constituted in a market economy is not the domain of the state. In this area, it is the entrepreneurs and managers who make the decisions. Yet the state is blamed for failures in the economy, from inflation to unemployment, and the parties involved in the game of 'changing of the guard's' play it in all seriousness. Of course, they get the credit if the economy prospers.

This division of functions between those who take the decisions and those 'responsible' politicians who legitimate them is simply continued within the state. Hence the term 'government responsibility' has a dual meaning. It signifies both responsibility for the condition of society at a given moment and responsibility for justifying the actions of civil servants and departments of state. Hence if a crisis occurs in the state or the economy, politicians are cast in the role of scapegoats.

Closer examination shows this fiction of the total responsibility of politics to be a complete illusion. Yet it is not kept in being only by the vanity of politicians, whose prestige is inflated by such pseudo-omnipotence, for there is no doubt that the state is being drawn ever more closely into the whole social process, thereby creating an impression of omnicompetence. Unfortunately, this is a 'totality from weakness' [22] arising from instrumentalization of the state by well-organized business interests and has little to do with political powers of decision or the ability to shape affairs.

Nevertheless it is the same trend towards totalization that renders the state administrations so opaque and uncontrollable; and this in turn promotes the separation of the machinery of state from politics, decision from legitimation, bureaucratic power from parliamentary responsibility.

The phenomenon in question is what Luhmann called 'the overtaxing of heads of organizations'. What happens is that organized power usually 'permits the formation of chains of considerable length and complexity, thus very quickly swamping the ability of the individual supremo to deal with the information flow and control the process'.[23] This leads Luhmann to make an early distinction between 'politics' and 'administration' in the sense that parties in government provide the administration with cover as regards legitimation, so that it can concentrate on the actual task of running the country. Thus a legitimation role is explicitly ascribed to politics.[24] Luhmann is quite happy about this situation. His diagnosis is certainly realistic, but he fails to take into account the consequences of this subservient role of politics in the industrial system, for it also creates a dilemma of legitimation of the parliamentary legitimators themselves, and the *de facto* freedom of action of administrations does nothing to increase the ability of government to govern.

The separation between the machinery of state and the institutions in the political arena which create legitimation cannot be sufficiently emphasized. It is quite fascinating to observe the extent to which the government machines of the Western industrialized countries have remained unaffected by the backwash of the crises of state legitimation experienced by those countries. The full weight of political disenchantment has fallen on the scapegoats in the political arena. Governments have been thrown out and replaced. Large-scale unemployment, government indebtedness, mistakes in energy planning, disasters in housing policy, environmental mishaps and unpopular decisions about armaments have all brought 'politics' into dire straits. In several countries the party system has got well and truly out of kilter. Ministers have been sacked. But the bureaucrats who did all the preparatory work, whose signatures got the minister into hot water, have survived each and every 'change of government'. No doubt about it, politics and administration are indeed two different things (Table 2)!

Table 2   Factors of unequal power in the state

Politics and politicians	Administration
Diffuse base (electors)	Specific base
Amateurism	Professionalism
Public action	Behind-the-scenes action
Need for legitimation	No need for legitimation
Short tenure	Usually a job for life
Small number of agents	Plethora of agents

It is true that policies initiated in the parliamentary framework do in fact have an important coordinating and smoothing function for government departments. Parliament also has built-in prerogatives, affecting the budget in particular, and the bureaucracy is formally dependent upon the decisions it takes. The reality of these institutional prerogatives, however, can be judged precisely by the budget and the extremely small difference it actually makes. This 'incrementalism', as Charles E. Lindblom calls it,[25] has been described in a study by Zimmermann and Müller on the Federal German Republic. According to them, there has been a steady decrease in the variation between expenditure in a number of categories, over the period 1963–78, and at the end of the period it amounted to hardly more than 1 per cent of central government expenditure averaged over the period.[26]

The great similarity between government budgets in Western industrialized countries also suggests either that negotiating margins are small or that very little use is made of them; it may also show that administrations copy the strategies of those in other countries or that their actions are motivated by similar considerations.

It is usual for politicians as political amateurs to be faced with highly specialized administrations, which can generally bank on the support of well-organized special interest groups (and their arguments). The staffs also enjoy all the advantages of preliminary discussions and decisions taken in private; they are under no constraint to prove their legitimacy, and do not have to fear for their jobs.

Most importantly, however, bureaucracies are themselves organizations of considerable strength with vested interests of their own. Indeed, these unequal quantities of politics and the machinery of state in themselves go far to explain the impotence of politics in the state, and why it can be treated as a mere instrument of the bureaucracy.

Take West Germany as an example. In 1984 the public service had 4.55 million employees, of whom 3.07 million were working directly for the federal and provincial governments. Their counterparts in the Federal and Land parliaments numbered 1,945 politicians. Thus on average each parliamentarian is supposed to use and control 1,573 public servants.[27] That might just be feasible. But the dilemma of most Western democracies is that the influence and control of parliament over the machinery of state passes through the needle eye of ministerial responsibility. There are 117 ministers in the Federal and Land parliaments. So, once more counting only direct employees of the central and provincial government, each minister presides over 26,239 civil servants![28] This single person has to carry 'governmental responsibility' for all of them. Their mistakes are his own, and he has to face the music alone.

On this point the change that has taken place can be quantified: since 1950 the number of public service employees in West Germany has doubled,[29] whilst the number of parliamentary deputies has remained almost unchanged. The history of parliament could be described as a steady deterioration of the control ratio between politics and the machinery of government.

Matters would be improved if government departments and the executive organs of the state were made directly answerable to parliament and subject to sanctions as their ministers in parliament are, but controlling and influencing the machinery of state in most Western democracies is a game played between politicians in parliament, from which the real protagonists are largely excluded. The minister plays the part of the administration *vis-à-vis* his colleagues in parliament.

The extent to which the pretence that politics decides, controls and is responsible for everything is taken seriously by those involved is nothing short of breathtaking. And the public gazes in fascination at the politicians in the spotlight of the political arena, for that is where all the black marks are handed out, when 'governmental responsibility' for what are obviously mistakes or abuses by civil servants has to be accepted. How the roles are distributed – here a scoundrel, there a celebrated politician – is something of a lottery, but it mainly depends upon the extent to which the conditions of all true role-playing are satisfied, namely that the expectations of the role partners should be fulfilled.

So the scapegoat role of politics in the industrialized countries of the West results firstly from the fact that the state decides little in the economy but has a hand in more and more affairs, and ends up by becoming responsible for everything. Secondly it arises in the state because the fiction that politics controls and decides provides a further argument for the total responsibility of politicians for the failures of the bureaucracy. Thirdly it arises because the mistakes of bureaucracies and industries that have become unmanageable have increased, thus creating a greater demand for scapegoats. 'Politics' is rewarded with considerable prestige for its willingness to take over this role.

Certainly it would be better if more responsibility were accorded to those who actually make the decisions, and more facilities for monitoring were accorded to those whom the decisions affect. But this is a vast field and would need an innovative thrust of formidable power in politics. As things are at present, 'the politicians' alone cannot be expected to generate such a thrust.

The countervailing power of the weakly organized public interest

Whatever may be thought of the details of this sketch of the power constellations, it furnishes a rational explanation of the universality of taboos on intervention. Nevertheless a self-help movement has come into existence in the shape of the alternative movement (or alternative trends) among the organizationally underprivileged. The growing number of protection interests has managed to create a perceptible counter-movement which, together with other forces making for change, has widened the decisional scope of politics. This is important in the overall nexus of events, and calls for explanation.

It is usual to distinguish two steering mechanisms in capitalist industrial systems – the market and the state. However, it has been observed that problems typical of industrial societies often meet with failure by the market to adapt and failures by state executives to take action. To the extent that such failures occur, a third quasi-steering entity comes into existence on the periphery of the political system. It arises mostly in connection with grievances outside the sphere of business or industry, where the interests involved do not readily lend themselves to organization. It is the work of critical citizens, consumers, lawyers or publicists who try as it were to get counter-action going on their own initiative.

The extent to which their protests, boycotts, lawsuits and attempts to form parties have borne fruit may in fact have been insufficient so far; all the same, in view of the impotent condition of politics it is of considerable importance, because this third level of control has a certain reflex action on the other two.

This third level is based on what were the residual resources of the constitutional parliamentary state.

These begin with the legal means of opposition. The external effects of industry have created grievances affecting increasingly powerful complainants. These grievances apply not simply to environmental and health interests, but in increasing numbers to property interests as well, for industrial expansion, including government policy on construction, has led to a gigantic process of expropriation (which would have unleashed a great deal of ideological indignation if it had been carried out in Eastern Europe). Indeed, in one lawsuit over a test facility for Daimler Benz, the case concerned expropriation by the state in favour of a private corporation. However, civil law and particularly the law on property also provide aids to fighting cases of this kind. Hence the process of annulling or dispossessing lower forms of ownership by higher ones is not effected with impunity.

The media too, torn between dependence on advertisers and purchasers and their love of the dramatic, offer certain resources. On several occasions the media by championing an aggrieved party have brought considerable political pressure to bear.

The third factor is political competition. When established political parties are in 'orderly' competition, some important social problems may well be successfully 'depoliticized'. In other circumstances, however, especially when new parties irrupt into the established party system with new themes, the structure of the political agenda may change considerably. In many Western Countries Green Parties have brought about such a change.

Without doubt an important factor favouring the countervailing power of weakly organized public interests was the fact that problems caused by industrialism affect people belonging to the governing classes, not perhaps as such but in other capacities and spheres of living: not in their ministerial suites, but in their residences or their favourite holidaying areas. This may well strengthen the hands of campaigning citizens when protests would otherwise have scant chance of gaining a hearing.

The widespread unease about the increasing danger of ecological breakdown has also led to an increased preparedness for change among the privileged classes and in the executive suites. The cumulative effect of all these disturbances is thus very great. It would be a grievous error, however, to imagine that some sort of self-correcting mechanism will come into play, as in the liberal theory of 'checks and balances'. Reliance on the self-correcting properties of 'critical public opinion', the rule of law in the state, inter-party competition and the 'pluralism' of the organized interests would be as misplaced as reliance on the self-correcting properties of the market, for the structural crisis in the Western industrial countries is due in large measure to the fact that all these liberal mechanisms are badly distorted. They may be sufficient for some forms of reactive policy, but in the long run preventive and anticipatory forms of policy are indispensable.

Only thoroughgoing innovations in society will avail to overcome the present 'institutionalized sclerosis', and the most important of these innovations will consist in comprehensively strengthening the decentralized level in the Western constitutional states adumbrated here and giving it entrenched institutional form. The parliamentary system is old, and it has often undergone institutional development during the course of its long history. One such reordering has now been overdue for decades.

3 The Theory of State Failure

Market failure and state failure

The theory of state failure arose as a response to the theory of market failure.[1] The theory of market failure was based on the proposition that the market is unable to satisfy certain types of demand, including the demands for law and order, universal education or fundamental research. According to Musgrave, whenever public goods are accessible to all, as are public highways or clean air, it is difficult for a public demand able to pay for it to be constituted – for who is going to pay if the desired good is available free of charge?

The market produces 'private' goods for an individual demand. The state offers 'public goods' for a collective demand. This is how the theory of market failure – which was intentionally confined to economic categories – explains the matter. The theory of state failure, which originates with Recktenwald and is likewise confined in the first instance to purely economic categories, now asks about the price of public goods, and here too it finds grounds for criticism.[2]

Recktenwald's diagnosis of state failure is confined to the fact of 'uneconomic performance in the state sector' (the title of his work). He is concerned with the profligate use made of tax revenues by public servants and with the excessive price of state services. The reasons for this inefficiency are set forth in a critique of bureaucracy from a market economy viewpoint. Reference is made to the problem of the separation between users of public goods and services and those who pay for them, to the absence of efficiency monitoring and of material incentives to efficiency in the administrative machine, to the cost consequences of the autonomous trade union organization of public servants, to the structural constraints on increased productivity, to the opaqueness of the budget mechanism and so on. One of Recktenwald's most important proposals for reform is entitled 'Denationalization'. I am even more critical about state failure, and that position concerns not only 'inefficiency *in* the state sector' but also the inefficiency of the state sector compared with the economy as a whole. It relates to the price and quality of the public goods, but it also relates to the problems of guidance within and outside the state sector, and to structural weaknesses in productivity and innovation of the public sector and within that sector.[3]

Even if state failure is referred to the theory of market failure, however, a more radical position emerges if certain naive assumptions of classical economics are left out, for in the industrial system of the West the state does not become involved simply because the market has no interest in certain goods.

For example, the state becomes involved when the market has an outlook that is too short-term and gives preference to the short-term interests of market participants over long-term interests.[4] In this case state failure means that the state too takes an excessively short-term view, not extending beyond the life of a parliament. The market is not concerned with the interests of the future or with preventive action to forestall problems. These are left to the state, and they increase the magnitude of the task which it will either perform or fail to perform.

The market also fails in the task of providing different groups or regions with similar living standards when they are of differing 'interest' to it. Public interests in general are its weak point, and they bring the state into play. This also happens because the market does not operate in the way that the Platonist model-builders of classical economic theory liked to think it does. The creation of monopolies, cartels and agreements of all kinds often stands the so-called 'laws of the market' on their head. They may for instance cause prices to rise at a time when sales are falling. The market is by no means self-perpetuating; indeed it has a constant tendency to abolish itself. This too brings the state into play, as in its policy on cartels.

The most important form of market failure, however, is that it generates externalities: it passes on costs and/or problems to the state and the community. In this case there is failure to allocate correctly the costs of and responsibilities for problems that have arisen, and this, like monopoly pricing, is a consequence of economic power accumulation processes. The very fact that demands arise for the 'internalization' of costs and responsibilities points to a failure of the market. The fact that over time these demands become increasingly frequent and clamant signals a failure by the state at this point.

Hence the market's lack of interest in particular goods is not the sole reason for the necessity of state action. Rather, it is the ill-effects of the market itself that create a need for 'public goods'.

The theory of state failure becomes radicalized in so far as it is appreciated that the state is bound to intervene to correct market failure; the need arises either from the nature of the market itself or from its preemption by monopolies. Therefore the champions of a pure market economy are poor counsellors in this matter, especially when they are after all the apologists for those who dominate the market – for the very forces whose influence is most responsible for the failure of the state.

Discussion of market failure and state failure remains unproductive as long as it is carried on by traditionalists of the classical economy or left-wing 'étatists'. The relationship between the market and the state is being redefined all over the world at the present time. The planned economies of Eastern Europe, for example, have increasingly had to recognize that basically the market performs an indispensable corrective function with regard to demand, price or productivity. At the same time the neo-classicists can no longer ignore the fact that the state is acquiring an increasingly important function in shaping the conditions within which the market must operate.

State activity as production

So salvation lies neither in choosing 'more market' or 'more state', nor in stepping up the production of 'public goods'. On the contrary, the challenge is to create conditions in which the market can operate with fewer problems, a situation which would reduce the demand for public goods.

This brings into view the fundamental point for a critique of the theories discussed here. It concerns the manner in which the state satisfies public requirements – the 'production' of public goods by specialized paid employees.

In principle, unhealthy conditions, inequalities, damage to the environment, traffic accidents and public or international insecurity can be avoided by political action – by structuring, by orders and prohibitions, and frequently by one-off cost-effective interventions at the origin of the causal chain creating the problem.

However, both the theory of market failure and that of state failure start out by assuming regular production of goods by the state. Musgrave says that the state either produces the public good itself or provides it. In the latter case the public good is produced privately but paid for by the state.[5]

This is the really interesting aspect of the theory of public goods. It does not take into account the political means available to the state of fulfilling its tasks by setting the scene and taking decisions. Instead it lays the emphasis on the production of public goods either by state employees in state-owned facilities or by industry. These are the crucial points on which the theory of state failure should concentrate. Recktenwald, by contrast, concentrates solely on the second point, production by the state and its excessive cost.

The concept of 'production' is highly relevant here. Let us assume that the state decided to have compliance with laws on the environment monitored partly by duly accredited groups of citizens. These groups would go into action if infringements occurred and would be able to call in the police or the courts if necessary. In this event the state would have to produce less of the good of 'clean air' in the form of government action. Clean air would then be produced more cheaply and, presumably, more effectively too. However, the state could also hand over the task of monitoring to a completely specialized bureaucracy. In this event the public good of a 'healthy environment' would be produced by bureaucratic means. This is production of which the not inconsiderable costs create incomes and contribute to the GNP, as do also the costs of the production of the good 'education' by teachers and the good 'health' by state hospitals. The incomes so earned are treated in GNP statistics as 'production sold'. In this case, however, it is not sold in the market: the price is paid via taxes or social insurance contributions.

Public goods are produced (1) by political regulation as intervention or structuring and (2) technocratically as 'production': (a) by the state, (b) by private industry directly at state expense and (c) by private industry indirectly at state expense (transfer payments). In 1987 state 'production' was valued at 11 per cent of GNP in West Germany. According to Musgrave, however, public goods include not only those produced by the state (2a) but also collective goods produced *privately* and paid for by the state (2b). In the more extended sense this also applies (2c) to privately produced goods and services financed via state transfer payments, e.g. the products of the health industry or the house building industry. Category (2c) includes not only the recipients of, say, housing subsidies or health insurance payments, but the final beneficiaries as well. The important fact is that goods actually produced by the state form only a small part of the public goods produced – and paid for.

Thus by far the greater part of the public goods about which market economy theorists speak is produced in such a way that incomes are generated, both in government departments and facilities and even more in private industry. Clearly the latter has become increasingly important in this connection. The state calls in private industry as a partner in the execution of its tasks, i.e. in the production of public goods, and pays the costs. By contrast, structural intervention in the performance of political tasks (1) is decreasing. Instead of structural measures being taken to solve problems, public money is flowing into the private sector. The 'denationalization' demanded by Recktenwald has long since begun. It takes the form of a tremendous 'economization' of state activity. It is also this which, together with the bureaucratization of state production of goods, makes the state so expensive and its products so unsatisfactory.

Stages in the failure of the state

If the tasks falling to the state are conceived as being primarily problem-led in response to demands from the community, one of the most evident signs of the poor quality of public goods is the *post facto* nature of the action taken, which amounts to combating symptoms rather than causes. This stems from failure to shape policies and take preventive action. I call it (a) political failure of the state, and in this I part company with Recktenwald.

The diseconomy of the excessive price of public goods produced by state and industry I term (b) economic failure of the state. This has to do with the efficiency of state activity. But since public goods generally exhibit structural inadequacies – substandard quality – in respect of the anticipated utility, we must also speak of (c) functional failure of the state, meaning the effectiveness of state activity.

Here we enter rough terrain full of paradoxes. The deplorable inefficiency of the state has causes rooted in the (market) economy. The proliferating bureaucracy is only a side-effect. This is the first paradox of the 'expensive state'.

Close behind comes the second paradox: the state does indeed fail in many of the tasks laid upon it by society; and yet it is acting 'economically' inasmuch as it creates incomes in problem areas of industrial society, at least in the short term.

The third paradox of the 'expensive state' is a somewhat disturbing one. The more money the state expends on dealing with problems caused by the industrial society, the more widely does it 'institutionalize' a lack of interest in taking preventive action to head off problems.

The fourth paradox lies in the self-reinforcing effect of failures by the state to intervene. The less the state takes preventive action and the more it carries out expensive remedial work after the event, the more strongly does its dependence on the tax dividends of the growth economy increase, in line with its need of finance. This in turn reinforces the 'hands-off industry' mentality.

The fifth paradox is the real problem: the antithesis between quantity and quality in the state. The enormous growth in state budgets and administrations is by no means a sign of political power (despite the considerable redistributive power of the bureaucracy); on the contrary it expresses the impotence of the state to which ample reference has already been made.

Quality and quantity

The state fails to intervene for the reasons given above. Its failure is visible to the naked eye in such phenomena as

1 the extent to which the state allows problems and costs to be passed on to it, even at the price of unconcealed financial and credibility crises,
2 the obsequiousness and the material incentives offered in order to attract private investment or to persuade industry to locate etc.,
3 the limited scope of intervention by national states with respect to the global market and the large groups operating in it,
4 the failure to take action even against state-owned public utilities.

But Leviathan's impotence can also be seen in the extent to which incomes are pocketed at problem points in the social process where the state, having neglected to take preventive measures, now has to deal with the consequences. This sector of the economy burgeoned spectacularly during the 1960s and 1970s. It is the phenomenon that O'Connor labelled the 'social–industrial complex' back in 1973 in his book *The Fiscal Crisis of the State*. This is in some sense the civilian counterpart of the military–industrial complex. But they have more than this in common. They both produce public goods for the state, military and civil. Thus both depend on government orders for their livelihood. Both make their habitat in the catchment area of state budgets. Both have a share in the tasks which fall to the state. Both do well out of the state's neglect to provide qualitative political solutions to problems. Neither of them has to woo the general public as consumers; they have the benefit of free advertising for public aims, provided that these are fulfilled by way of the state-financed production of public goods. These modern 'court suppliers' of the parliamentary system have opened up the civil objectives of the state as an enormous 'market' – a market which offers several advantages over the real market, from greater predictability to the prices that can be obtained (see p. 14).

What particularly interests me about all this is that this type of economic activity is especially prevalent wherever the conditions and consequences of the socioeconomic process generate problems that have not been forestalled by preventive action. For example, the unchecked avalanche of cars makes road building imperative, just as unhealthy conditions in industry promote the growth of large-scale ecological or medical industries in a cycle involving the supply of goods followed by the supply of remedies for the problems they cause.[7]

Inherent in this process is a tendency for quantity to displace quality as an aspect of the production of public goods. Just as the quality of international relations takes second place when external security is sought primarily through the production of armaments, so too in the civilian sector the quality aspect falls into neglect.

Take as an example internal security. From 1965 to 1985 the number of crimes per 100,000 inhabitants in West Germany rose from 3,000 to nearly 7,000, whilst the percentage of cases cleared up fell from 53.2 to 47.2. Yet in the same period expenditure on public safety there rose from 3,000 million DM to 16,500 million DM.[8] With this money 50 per cent more public servants were paid in the security services, prisons were built and the equipment and buildings of the police forces were constantly improved. This unsolved problem also provided not only copy for the mass circulation press but also a livelihood for private security services and for manufacturers of all kinds of security equipment. So the problem was paid for once via the state and then again privately.

Yet with all this growth in quantity there was little public discussion of the causes of criminality. In no sphere has prevention been so neglected as in this one, a circumstance which points to the magnitude of state failure in this area. Whatever may be the reasons for so much criminality, they have their origin in the quality of relations within society. Yet this is an area largely avoided by the state.[9]

Educational problems, too, are first and foremost qualitative in nature. However, the widely deplored catastrophe in education unleashed a flurry of quantitative growth: first of staff, and then in the relevant sectors of the social–industrial complex. In all this, educational policy featured mainly as policy on building schools and colleges, and it is currently largely concerned with the provision of technical aids to education.

Again, the emphasis in policy on research is placed on technical inventions which can be developed for quantity production. The most neglected field is that of social discoveries and institutional innovation – the field of quality. Thus it is evident that objective of 'quantitative growth' is not confined to production in private industry. The same emphasis is discoverable in the goods and services provided by the state.

Combating symptoms

The significance of the social–industrial complex stems primarily from the symbiosis between bureaucracy and industry in connection with specific activities of the state. As was stated earlier, the state calls upon private enterprise for assistance in discharging its many duties. Usually the state also sees to the financing, either from the public budget or through arrangements whereby private entities undertake to make payments. This creates situations of private interest and gives the department of state concerned a clientele which strengthens its position in the contest for influence and budget share. Thus the state and the clientele together acquire a considerable power of definition with regard to the strategy to be adopted by the state (see p. 15ff).

Whoever gives state bureaucracies any say in dealing with the consequences of problems caused by industry should be aware that the two sides are more likely to form a partnership than to adopt a conflictual relationship. This is not primarily because of the illegitimate exercise of influence by way of all kinds of corruption and 'perks', although these are not negligible. Nor is it because the chiefs on either side have similar interests and standards of living and are more likely to get on well with one another than with plebeian folk. What really tends to tip the scale is that bureaucracies and industries are structurally similar. By outlook and by the set of their interests, they both tend to favour a strategy of combating symptoms, in that

1 both are organized on a pattern of central control and division of labour,
2 both prefer global routine solutions, analagous to mass production,
3 both tend to take action at the end of the chain of causation where problems are visible, prolific and calculable,
4 both state and industrial technocracies have similar economic interests – the former is interested in getting a larger budget allocation and the latter in extending its markets.

These structural affinities lead to technocratic definitions of problems, which

1 disregard the variety and complexity of problems, because of specialization,
2 do not inquire into the causes of problems, but combat the symptoms,
3 reject one-off non-routine cheap interventions in favour of expensive standardized measures,
4 in short, close their eyes to preventive measures involving structural policy in favour of *post facto* nuisance abatement.[10]

The propensity of both bureaucratic and industrial social technocracies to define problems in this way is compounded by their combined powers of definition. Faced with such powers, political decision-makers are at a great disadvantage. Consequently, the growth of social technocracies contributes to the unmanageability of the industrial system.

This preference for symptom-combating strategies is fraught with consequences. In the first place, such strategies are directed solely at the highly visible symptoms. Problems that have not yet impinged on the public consciousness tend to be neglected. Furthermore, the conspicuous symptoms tend to be tackled in isolation. In the case of power stations, for example, in addition to the special dust filters and noise-reducing equipment, separate large installations are built to combat the pollutants sulphur dioxide and nitrogen oxides.

This alone is enough to make the results of these strategies expensive, but they are particularly expensive if the causes, still unchecked, are on the increase, for then expenditures on accident reduction on the highways, the reduction of toxic emissions or the imprisonment of criminals do not prevent the symptoms from regaining their former levels and thus eventually necessitating fresh countermeasures.

However, this attitude most commonly results in problems simply being displaced, or in what I call 'technocratic iatrogenesis'.[11] Iatrogenesis is the induction of illness by the physician. It has a significant incidence in the health field in the form of medicines which cause illness, unnecessary operations or clinical infections. In the metaphorical sense it can be seen in other fields as well. For example, prisons are usually universities of crime, and many a 'criminal career' was first planned in such institutions. In foreign affairs security, viewed as resulting from additional armaments, usually engenders more insecurity in the shape of a fresh arms spurt by the adversary. In environmental protection with a nuisance abatement bias, environmental problems are commonly reintroduced by staving them off until later (see p. 47ff).

Not the least of the faults of the symptom-combating strategy is that it serves as a substitute for innovation. The pressure is temporarily taken off the technology or the social structure which needs to be changed. Some might think it better to use the money for providing a more innovative and appropriate solution. Alas, such solutions are frequently a last resort, adopted only after crises have demonstrated that the world market is demanding a fresh solution or because the symptom-combating strategy is no longer affordable.

This point has been reached in many Western countries and the question is whether and to what extent the effects of the crisis will at last lead to the adoption of more appropriate, economical and effective solutions. To investigate this question in greater detail it is useful to examine three areas more closely.

(1) In the area of health and environmental protection political failure by the state has now become manifest in the shape of extensive abandonment of preventive action. Economic failure by the state consists principally in the fact that expenditure on health places a specially heavy burden on the public finances without very much to show for the increase. At the same time the health service has become the largest sector of industry in the industrial countries, a sector which gives rise to substantial problems of control and management. In this connection one of the most significant aspects of environmental protection is that it is a form of preventive medicine, but it will not exert its full preventative effect until even environmental protection is not the final arbiter.

(2) This is why the areas of traffic, energy and structural policy have to be examined. The point of interest in these areas, as also in policy in building or agriculture, is prevention in the field of health and the environment, but they are also of interest because, owing to the lack of structural solutions, they possess at the same time a large potential for economic and/or fiscal crises. In any event they provide good illustrations of the impotence of politics in encounters with large industrial concerns.

(3) Government debt has become chronic in most Western countries since 1970, and will remain so until the 1990s. It is a flagrant demonstration of the failure of such states, whether or not one considers government debt a bad thing in principle (which incidentally I do not). States which over a period of 20 years fail to bring their revenue and expenditure into balance are falling down on their own job, and adding the cost of interest to the price tag on their public goods. This is political state failure in the form of failure to curb the excessive revenues paid to vested interests. It is functional state failure, whether in financial planning or in efficient expenditure controls. It is economic state failure, because this process makes the state even more expensive and restricts its financial room for manoeuvre. And there is a smug third party who does well out of all this in close cooperation with the government finance departments – the banking sector.

4 Public Health and Protection of the Environment

Curative medicine

The state fails significantly with regard to health under the three aspects previously mentioned:

1 politically, through failure to take adequate preventive measures,
2 economically, in the shape of uneconomic costly methods of production, and
3 functionally, by reason of the relatively inefficient nature or deficient quality of the product (see p. 35).

The health service has attracted criticism most of all for being uneconomic. In nearly every Western country health services are provided predominantly as public goods and services, an exception being the United States. More accurately, they are produced privately for the greater part, but are financed mostly from public funds. This production occupies a sector of the economy which in many industrial countries has outstripped all other sectors in importance.

Moreover, the sector is growing rapidly. Whereas in 1960 Western countries spent on average some 4.2 per cent of their annual economic output (GNP) for health purposes, by 1970 such expenditure had risen to 5.7 per cent and by 1983 to 7.6 per cent.[1] In the United States the share was nearly 11 per cent.[2] (Here and in subsequent chapters GNP is used in order to provide an internationally comparable representation of orders of magnitude; it does not furnish actual quotas.)

In West Germany expenditure on health from the government's social security budget rose from 31,000 million DM in 1965 to 192,000 million DM in 1985, or some 10.4 per cent of GNP (table 3). The social security budget does not even include all that is spent on health. For if we include the private

Table 3   Expenditure on health in the social security budget and cases
of unfitness for work and hospitalization in state insurance

	Health expenditure from social security budget		Unfitness for works (per 100 members)[a]		Hospital cases (per 100 members)	
Year	milliard DM	Percentage of GNP	Men	Women	Men	Women
1965	31	6.8	70.7	65.5		
1968	39	7.3	69.9	69.5		
1970	52	7.6	89.0	86.5	9.4	12.2
1973	82	8.9	98.6	95.0	10.3	13.0
1975	107	10.3	85.5	85.8	11.1	14.0
1978	133	10.3	99.3	95.7	13.3	16.5
1980	158	10.6	103.2	96.7	13.7	16.6
1983	171	10.2	85.5	84.3	14.3	17.5
1985	192	10.4	93.0	92.6	15.6	18.8

[a]Excluding pensioners and students.
Source: Statistical Yearbook of the Federal German Republic and the Federal Ministry for Labour and Social Order, Social Report for the year stated

expenditure not shown here (households and insurances) and a portion of the state payments for health purposes that does not form part of the social security budget, then the figure for 1985 is 241,500 million DM or 13.1 per cent of GNP![3]

In 1981 this proportion of the total cost of health provision was nearly 13.4 per cent of GNP. The reduction resulted from a cost containment policy which made little difference to the overall structure, the privileges and the vested interests of the 'medical–industrial complex', the main result being to make people pay more. For this reason, in 1985 costs began to rise again as a proportion of GNP,[4] and they have now necessitated a third cost containment reform in 1988. Most experts agree that it will not be the last.

When one reflects that by far the greater part of this avalanche of costs has to be borne by employees and employers, one is left wondering at the small amount of health that was 'bought' with this huge economic potential. Although the number of workers absent through sickness usually shows a sharp decline in times of large-scale unemployment such as the present, the figures for the 1980s are higher than those for the 1960s when health was even 'cheaper'. The number of hospital cases is continuously rising.

The health status of the population as a whole was, to say the least, remarkably unaffected by the deluge of costs lavished on the medical sector. At all events, the proportion of sick and injured West German citizens in 1982 was 16.3 per cent, exactly the same as it had been in 1974, whilst the percentage of the chronically sick is high and rising.[5]

Improvements in health care such as occurred during the 1970s seem to have led to increased life expectancy in most Western countries. However, closer examination reveals that this success is largely a gratis effect, i.e. an unearned bonus for the health industry.

To whom were these gratis effects due? In previous decades general hygiene has played an important part. More recently increased leisure and recreation, informative articles and programmes on medical topics in the media or widespread self-medication are likely to have reinforced the trend.

Furthermore, the reduction in heavy industrial work resulting from the trend to quality-intensity has indisputably had a favourable effect on life expectancy. Research carried out in France shows a difference of nearly nine years in the life expectancy of 35-year-old males, depending on their occupation, and industrial occupations are at the lower end, with service occupations enjoying a much better prognosis.[6] A more pronounced 'post-industrial' structure of occupations is reflected in correspondingly longer life expectancy.

Then there is the exodus from the inner cities, whilst protection of the environment provides another gratis effect for public health. Granted that the policy of tall factory chimneys is not a complete answer to the problem of pollution (see p. 47), it has nevertheless resulted in decreased atmospheric pollution levels in several congested areas in industrial countries. Research has shown that such a decrease can lengthen life expectancy by several years.[7] As far as I am aware, empirical data on international comparisons of atmospheric pollution and life expectancy seem to indicate that countries and cities with less atmospheric pollution also have on average a higher comparative life expectancy, other living conditions being equal.[8]

Thus there are many aspects of living not directly influenced by the expensive health system yet contributing to its better performance. Further progress would seem to depend simply on taking energetic action along the lines indicated, but that is the simple solution that is hard to implement. True, there has of late been widespread discussion of the insufficiency of purely curative medicine which leaves out of account the socially conditioned nature of the pathology profile in industrial countries ('the ills of civilization').[9] Nevertheless the overwhelming proportion of the enormous expenditures on health continues to be invested in the treatment of cases of sickness. In 1985 a bare 6 per cent of all health expenditure in West Germany was devoted to 'preventive treatment',[10] and even these sums were largely spent to measures such as early diagnosis, protective inoculation and other items in the foreground of curative medicine.

Unlike the structure of illnesses in the developing countries, sickness in the industrial countries is no longer predominantly a matter of infections. Here the illnesses are influenced in the main by stress factors and environmental risks, disregarding for the moment the change in the age structure.[11] Obviously it is easier for the health authorities to combat bacteria and viruses than to take action about conditions in society which induce illness.

The Organization for Economic Cooperation and Development (OECD) also agrees with other writers on the subject 'that non-medical factors . . . are more important determinants of health than the health service'.[12] No doubt what the OECD has mainly in mind here is unhealthy conduct by individuals such as smoking or drinking rather than social conditions which tend to encourage such behaviour or those conducive to passive morbidity such as stress at work, noise or a polluted environment. Even this restricted view leads the OECD to the conclusion 'that additional health measures would do little if anything to change the mortality or morbidity'.[13]

That is the crucial point. As long as health policy fails to concern itself with non-medical factors, and in so far as it neglects social preventive measures, though it may help to alleviate suffering here and there it will have little influence on the structure of morbidity or mortality. Thus the hiatus between the costs of health provision and the health of the people may persist for a long time.

Nothing demonstrates this more clearly than a comparison of the levels of life expectancy in industrial countries. In 1984 the leading group contained Iceland, Japan and Norway, countries where expenditure on health services is in the middle range, but in addition Sweden and Holland, which spend much more on health. West Germany and the United States, which spend in all more than 10 per cent of GNP on health, are only in the middle band of Western industrial countries with regard to life expectancy.[14] All in all, this shows an astonishing lack of results from a gigantic input of economic resources.

Environmental protection as end-of-pipe treatment

As was said earlier, protection of the environment is a form of preventive health policy, but it is quite incommensurate with the colossal expenditure undertaken in the health sector. In 1985 state and industry spent 1.4 per cent of GNP on protection of the environment in West Germany.[15] In the Western industrial countries these expenditures average from less than 1 to 1.8 per cent (in United States), whilst in Japan they have at times been higher.

The percentages may be small, but the absolute amounts spent every year on environmental protection are still enormous. In West Germany they totalled 186,000 million DM from 1975 to 1984.[16] In the United

States $435,000 million were spent from 1972 to 1982.[17]

Moreover, a not inconsiderable number of people make their living from the problems of the environment. The IFO Institut für Wirtschaftsforschung calculates that in West Germany the number has been growing steadily ever since 1970, amounting to 433,000 in 1984. During recent years the ecology industry has had exceptionally good sales figures, and its growth prospects are generally reckoned to be good.[18]

However, protection of the environment had become established as a new policy area as early as the beginning of the 1970s. Japan was the first country to enact comprehensive laws on the environment, in 1967 and 1970, and was followed by Sweden in 1969, whilst the United States and East Germany both did so in 1970.[19] West Germany promulgated a comprehensive programme for the protection of the environment in 1971. Thus enough time has now elapsed for the effects of the measures taken to be assessed. The degree of success achieved by state environmental policies has differed from one country to another. Taking the important aspect of keeping the air clean, the picture is as follows. Up to 1985 the most extensive successes had been achieved in Japan. The 'pioneers' Sweden and the United States, together with Luxembourg, Holland, Norway, Switzerland and Austria, are in the upper third. In the middle range are Western Europe including West Germany and (lower down) the United Kingdom, followed by southern and Eastern Europe, where in some places even elementary forms of environmental protection are lacking. All in all, no country has so far developed anything like an adequate environmental protection programme. Nevertheless, the relative differences between the above-mentioned groups are of interest because the intensity of the efforts made to improve the environment is also a reliable indicator of a country's potential for innovation.

Let us now take a closer look at West Germany, as the representative country for the upper middle range. What successes have been achieved in its policy on the environment? The answer might be schematized as follows: (a) partial successes with regard to symptoms, based largely on (b) problem displacement or (c) gratis effects, counteracted by (d) the cost of damage running into milliards and serious cost–benefit imbalances resulting from (e) the neglect of preventive measures and (f) little innovative effect.

PARTIAL SUCCESSES AND OPTICAL ILLUSIONS

Life expectancy of both people and trees is comparatively short in West Germany. According to recent OECD data the number of species endangered there is particularly high.[20] Dying forest trees, periods of smog in the winter of 1984–5 and 1986–7, the pollution of water by nitrates, the increasing contamination of drinking water, the pollution of the Rhine by chemicals in 1986, the deaths of robins in 1988, toxic waste problems and the serious contamination of the ground, all tend to suggest that the state has failed in this area.

Yet there have been improvements in environmental protection. In some cases considerable decreases in the high concentrations of pollution in industrial areas have been recorded – emissions of lead, suspended dust, carbon monoxide and sulphur dioxide decreased.[21] Nor is this without significance. One result is that in most of the heavily polluted regions the trend of life expectancy has shown an improvement over the values recorded in the 1960s. Moreover, indicators of biological oxygen demand (BOD) have pointed to a lessening of water pollution. In this respect by 1985 the situation of the Rhine had improved as much as that of the Seine or the Mississippi.[22]

Even in these showcases of conventional environmental protection, however, the number of unsolved problems is legion. From just the strictly technocratic viewpoint, which usually measures only successes resulting from specific action, the decrease in water and air pollution turns out to be an optical illusion. In respect of air purification the problems of nitrogen oxide and of photochemical oxidants had remained unsolved in West Germany and in most of the industrial countries, at least until 1986. To them are added the problems of 'new' toxic substances which hitherto have received little attention because they occur in small quantities and in specific localities, although they can in fact be even more harmful.

The achievements of the biological sewage purification plants in water pollution abatement are a gain. Against this, however, the rivers are becoming increasingly polluted with nitrates and the situation of still waters is even worse. The OECD report on the environmental situation in Western countries, which is very critical, contains a reference to increasing problems of quality of drinking water.[23] In waste disposal, too, partial successes are balanced by problems with toxic wastes, which seem to be on the increase.

In environmental noise protection, partial improvements by means of protective walls on motorways, or quieter aircraft, have not sufficed to prevent the situation from worsening. Sixteen per cent of the population in the Western industrial countries are exposed to 'unacceptable' noise conditions, and a further 34 per cent are injuriously affected by noise; and this proportion of the population is increasing.[24] The most potent cause of the situation is the ever-growing volume of mass motorization and road freight traffic. Clearly, military noise is also on the increase, not least in over-militarized West Germany.[25]

And the further we move from the traditional areas of environmental protection, the worse is the overall situation. In land protection efforts to prevent further pollution by toxins or buildings have failed almost completely,[26] despite the extension of nature reserves of which, however, West Germany has comparatively few.

Thus, protection of the environment has been successful only in limited sectors in most of the Western industrial countries, even at the level of combating symptoms. It has not so far managed to solve a large part of the problems addressed, or to prevent new symptoms from appearing. This is inherent in the nature of the technocratic approach to combating symptoms, which flits from one toxin to another and, provided sufficient public money is made available, attacks them with special regulations, bureaucracies, measuring systems or cleansing plants. As long as the causative agents of these vast amounts of pollution – road traffic, the energy, chemicals and building industries, or the military – are 'no go' areas for intervention, this 'first aid' form of environmental protection will have to chase after the symptoms in a purely reactive mode.

The full extent of state failure to protect the environment becomes apparent only on a closer examination of the partial successes achieved in combating symptoms, for with respect to air and water purification, apart from gratis effects these have very largely relied simply on problem displacement.

PROBLEM DISPLACEMENT

Problem displacement means simply shifting a problem from one medium or place to another – from water into the air or the ground, from densely populated areas to mountainous regions, or from industrial countries to the Third World (as at Bhopal). Hence problem displacement in the field of environmental protection only creates fresh problems.

For example, the 7,800 sewerage purification plants in West Germany not only take up a great deal of surface area and create problems of smell, they also produce 2.1 million tonnes (dry weight) of sewage sludge. In the Western countries deposits of sewage sludge rose by 50 per cent between 1975 and 1980.[27] Some of this was disposed of in special incineration plants, thus polluting the air once more.

A large amount of toxic wastes from sewerage plants is sunk in the sea. In the course of time this form of ocean pollution has reached significant proportions. Even as refuse to be deposited, these wastes constitute a problem. In the same way, flue gas desulphurization installations cause problems of waste and its transportation. They produce formidable quantities of gypsum. According to official West German statistics, in 1988 these amounted to 2.9 million tonnes, destined to rise to 3.5 million tonnes by 1993.[28] Clean air filter waste also contains a variety of toxic heavy metals. Refuse incineration plants, as an aspect of waste disposal, constitute a new and massive environmental problem by the considerable pollution of the air that they cause. There is no doubt that the death of the forest resulting from the 'high chimneystacks' policy is a peculiarly tragic aspect of problem displacement. The flaws in such a policy have been evident for years.

I warned about this in 1976, receiving a formal contradiction by an oil company, followed by one from the Federal Office of the Environment itself. What I said then about sulphur dioxide pollution, which was contested at the time, was still applicable even in the early 1980s and will bear citation: 'The high concentrations in the densely populated areas are decreasing, but the emissions are causing an *increase* in pollutant concentration in areas remote from industry, and the . . . quantity of sulphur dioxide discharged into the air each year between Prague and Liverpool continues to increase, as complaints from Norway and Sweden become more frequent since these clouds of sulphur dioxide are deposited in the form of acid rain. Up to the present our efforts to protect the environment have resulted, at least in continental Europe, only in improved organization of the distribution of these pollutants . . . whereas emission-reducing production processes appear to have had little effect so far.'[29]

Local concentrations of harmful substances, then, have been curbed with varying success, but emissions fatal to forests – sulphur dioxide and nitrogen oxide (see figure 2) – are still high. Above all, at power stations little had changed by 1983. Even in 1986 nitrogen oxides in West Germany were at a higher level than they had been in 1970. The same applies to traffic on the roads, where until 1986 both nitrogen oxide and organic compounds showed an increase.[30] Both power station operators and the car industry were astonishingly free from state intervention under environmental policy for a long time. The most vigorous effort by the state went into clean air regulation of private households, and it was here that the improvement was most marked – illustrating once again that failure by the state always has some connection with positions of strength.

GRATIS EFFECTS

Whereas nitrogen oxide emissions in West Germany and elsewhere were still on the increase, sulphur dioxide emissions were decreasing at the end of the period. However, figure 2 shows that even this effect was not (until 1983) produced primarily by clean air regulations. It was due mainly to energy saving and the low rate of economic growth – the former being a reaction to the high cost of fuel! In other words, without the further sharp rise in energy costs in 1979 and the consequent constraint on energy consumption, SO_2 emissions would not have decreased either. Even the United States, which spends more on protection of the environment, did little more than register these gratis effects.

In Japan, by contrast, the energetic prosecution of environmental protection combined with an effective energy-saving policy had more far-reaching effects, most notably by clean-up measures up to 1975, and thereafter by

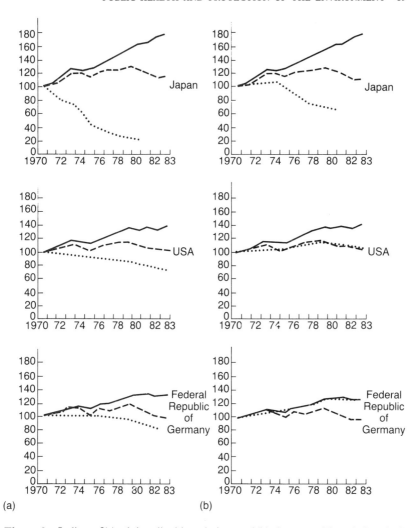

Figure 2 Indices of (a) sulphur dioxide emissions and (b) nitrogen oxide emissions (....) compared with gross domestic product (——) and consumption of fossil fuels (---).
Source: OECD, *The State of the Environment 1985*, Paris 1985, pp. 23, 25.

energy saving. Unlike flue gas desulphurization installations with their high operating costs, the environmental protection afforded by energy saving has the advantage of being largely self-financing because less fuel is purchased.

The largest gratis effect in environmental protection in many Western countries was caused by the structural depression in the 'smokestack industries'. Apart from countries such as Japan or Sweden, this change was not really due to a policy purposely adopted by the state. On the contrary, as a structural crisis with enormous social costs (as in the United Kingdom) it signalized a conspicuous failure on the part of the state, and a lack of foresight. These gratis effects of structural changes on environmental and health policy point unmistakably to the need for the state to adopt structural policies commensurate with the situation (see p. 65ff).

THE COST OF DAMAGE

The economic justification for the protection of the environment is that it avoids or reduces the costs occasioned by damage to the environment. Thus the level of costs for unprevented damage quantifies the failure of the state in this respect.

However inadequate the estimates of the cost of damage to the environment may be, there is widespread agreement that such expenditure exceeds the amount that would have been spent on prevention. The OECD has on several occasions estimated the cost of damage to the environment since 1979 at 3–5 per cent of GNP[31] for the industrial countries of the West. No doubt these estimates should be treated with reserve. Professor Wicke of the Federal Office of the Environment estimates that the figure for West Germany is at least 6 per cent.[32] When compared with the actual current expenditure of 1–2 per cent of GNP on protection of the environment, they show the extent to which the main weight of expenditure has hitherto been directed towards repairing the damage. They also indicate clearly that problems of the environment place a much heavier burden on economies than the sums actually devoted to environmental protection would suggest.

Consider air pollution for instance. Research in some Western countries has shown that in 1978 this caused damage to the extent of between 1 and 2 per cent of GNP. These were the costs of sickness and damage to buildings, the land, plants and materials caused by airborne pollutants. It has been calculated that in the United States the costs of damage avoided by clean air measures in 1977 were of the order of 1.2 per cent of GNP.[32] For 1978 it was estimated that a reduction of 20 per cent in dust and sulphur dioxide pollution alone saved the United States damage costs of the order of 1 per cent of GNP. Such expenditures are naturally higher in densely populated areas that are polluted. In Athens, air pollution causes damage evaluated at about $200 million every year.[34]

By far the greater proportion of such outlays is spent on health. It has been estimated that even a 20 per cent reduction in pollution of the air by sulphur dioxide and dust would enable the savings shown in table 4 to be made.

Table 4   Savings on health expenditure from reduction in SO_2 and dust in 1978

Country	Savings (millions)	Savings per capita in 1978 (US$)
United States	$17,000	78.4
United Kingdom	£640	54.0
France	8,200 f	30.1
Netherlands	900 fl	60.5
Norway	40 Kr	5.5

Source: *Wirtschaft und Umwelt* No. 4, 1983, p. 20

The asbestos industry in the United States provides a striking example of the cost of the damage caused in the health field alone. In that country over 30,000 lawsuits have been brought by people suffering the effects of asbestos, with claims totalling thousands of millions of dollars, even leading to upsets in the insurance market.[35]

In addition to health damage, forest destruction has now reached alarming proportions both in central Europe and the United States. The costs so occasioned have increased sharply in West Germany since 1980. Berlin Technical University has calculated that in future this damage alone is likely to cost between 5,500 and 8,800 million DM every year.[36] Tasks such as land cleaning, the 'inherited burdens' of inappropriately stored toxic wastes and the processing of drinking water also call for considerable expenditure. In these areas, too, rehabilitation costs are set to rise rather than fall.

NEGLECT OF PREVENTIVE MEASURES

It is in prevention that the state fails most signally in the field of pollution control. This is failure at the level of structuring, as opposed to failure of the 'production' of public environmental goods. To clarify this failure by the state, we need to differentiate between possible strategies for the environment. I distinguish four stages.

First, the most primitive form is simple *repair* or reinstatement when damage to the environment has occurred. This is the stage at which environmental policy usually begins to act.

The second stage consists of *post facto* nuisance-abating environmental protection. It 'retrofits' a production, consumption or transport system that is basically hostile to the environment with supplementary equipment that reduces damage to the environment. Such equipment includes filtering units, sewage purification plants, waste incinerators, noise reduction walls, measuring equipment and other products of the ecology industry and its symptom-curing devices.

The third stage of policy on the environment aims at an *ab initio* environmentally safe technology, mostly one which economizes on resources as well. It favours innovations that introduce more appropriate technology rather than cosmetic supplements to an industrial structure that is basically hostile to the environment. It is the stage of ecologically motivated innovations or of ecological modernization.[37]

The fourth stage of environmental policy aims at structural change. No longer is it sought to improve ecologically inappropriate technologies or economic activities by supplementary action or innovation. The aim is rather to activate structural change leading to the 'post-industrial' production methods of the services and information sectors or to modes of travel that are inherently less hostile to the environment, such as public transport. I should like to illustrate these four stages by taking forest destruction as an example.

Stage 1 would consist of repairing or making good damage to forests.
Stage 2 would consist of installing flue gas cleansing devices in power stations and fitting existing cars with exhaust catalysers.
Stage 3 would be the technical optimization of the energy system in order to achieve greater economy in the use of primary energy and optimization of the combustion process in energy-saving car engines.
At stage 4 there would be a structural change to more energy-saving modes of production and consumption, and to a structure of transport that would as a minimum result in fewer vehicle kilometres being driven.

Environmental strategies 1 (repair) and 2 (nuisance abatement) in pollution control are at the symptom-combating level. Strategies 3 (ecological modernization) and 4 (structural change) are at the prevention level.

Depending on circumstances there will always be a mixture of these strategies (e.g. because there is a greater disposition to effect repairs at later stages than at earlier stages and because a certain amount of nuisance abatement will be indispensable). Nevertheless it is a characteristic of the situation that at present we are mainly moving from stage 1 to stage 2. We are trying to progress from repairing the damage to forests, which is scarcely possible, to flue gas cleansing by way of 'add-on' environmental technology, leaving the technology and structure of the energy system and of road transport as such untouched.

LIMITED INNOVATIVE EFFECT

The state might reasonably have been expected to aim for one effect in particular with its policy on the environment, namely to stimulate technical progress towards ecologically more advantageous innovation and modernization: in other words, to pursue strategy 3. So what innovative effect has environmental policy had so far? In the United States the proportion invested in the 'add-on' type of environmental technologies compared with investment in *ab initio* 'cleaner' technologies remained almost constant from 1973 to 1983 at the relatively high percentage of 77. In West Germany the proportion invested in 'add-on' environmental technology compared with environment-friendly product or process innovations was about 70 per cent in 1975 and had actually increased to 74 per cent by 1980.[38] For Japan there are only incomplete data from the early phase of environmental protection in that country. During this period (1971–5) less was spent on environment-friendly technology than in the United States and West Germany. Unlike those two countries, however, such expenditures rose rapidly, a fact which the Japanese Office of the Environment singled out for praise as early as 1976.[39] Studies from the Berlin Scientific Centre also record a plethora of the usually cost-intensive 'add-on' processes of the first stage, with the recycling process for refuse and waste water indicating a more favourable trend. In fact the norm is still to use purely 'add-on' devices rather than integrated solutions specific to the production process.[40]

CONCLUSION

After nearly 20 years the failure of environmental protection based on combating symptoms is plain to see. In some cases, such effects as have been recorded were achieved largely by redistributing the pollution, whilst others were to a significant degree not attributable to environmental protection measures but caused instead by the depression in the smokestack industries, the high cost of energy and a slowdown in the growth of the economy. In view of the environmental problems that were left unsolved and the new ones that arose, the costs were far too high. They cannot be justified even by saying that at least they led to some diminution in the high cost of damage to the environment.

In the 1980s the crisis in the nuisance abatement and repair types of environmental protection has created strong pressure for change in Western countries. The need to look ahead and to plan comprehensively for protection of the environment is being stressed, as it was in the early 1970s. The 'polluter-pays' principle is once again in vogue, as is 'qualitative growth'. In the West German Social Democratic Party (the SPD) the formula of 'ecological modernization' put into currency in 1982 by the author is heard once more.[41] Under the menace of dying forests West Germany has been stimulating action by the EEC in the matter of policy on the environment, and now even Mrs Thatcher has been converted to the Green cause.

But protection of the environment really affecting polluters such as power stations and road vehicles is something that Japan began 15 years ago. There is no clearer sign of 'Eurosclerosis' than this long time-lag.

5 Transport and Energy Policy

Transport policy

'The car is . . . safety and pollution problem number one! The car does more to pollute the environment than any other means of transport. The car creates most of the noise problems. The car requires the greatest surface area for its movement and parking. With the exception of air transport, the car consumes the largest amount of energy per person. The car poses the greatest risk of accident to all of us. The car is even a problem when it is no longer running.'[1]

That description came from the West German Federal Office of the Environment. Why does just one means of transport constitute a problem of these proportions? Why can the state not step in and take preventive action to lessen the problem? The Office of the Environment itself gives the answer straightaway: 'The car is more than an important means of travel and transport; it is also an important factor in the economy. The automobile industry is a "key industry" of our economy, not only because of its own economic importance but also because of the close links it has with other branches of the economy such as the steel industry, the chemical and electrical engineering industries, and the rubber and textile industries . . . one job in every seven in the Federal Republic is directly or indirectly dependent on the car.'[2] This is indeed a position of strength, and the state is loath to interfere with it.

- This is evident with regard to speed limits, as the examples given later will show.
- It is evident in the special regime of taxes and allowances, which will be described in the next chapter.
- It is very evident from the fact that, like the producers of electricity, the automobile industry was but little affected by the steps taken in the 1970s to

protect the environment. Between 1970 and 1986 pollution by nitrogen oxide and organic compounds from road traffic, which was already high, increased.[3]

But the automobile industry also provides an example of how lamentably such failure to intervene can discourage the propensity of an industry to innovate. Power with its attendant special treatment lessens the pressure to innovate (see p. 109). Conversely, experience in Japan has shown that state intervention in the public interest can be a powerful stimulant to innovation. The Japanese example also makes it clear that industrial power need not necessarily be the final determinant of the state's freedom of manoeuvre, and that there are also political techniques in dealing with it, provided that the necessary conditions exist for the state to take an active role.

However, an innovative role adopted by the state can create considerable difficulties for the cognate industries in other countries. In this case the question of employment becomes reversed. The American automobile industry, which had been constantly increasing the fuel consumption of its models until 1973–4, was brought near to collapse in the early 1980s by its stubborn neglect of energy saving.[4] In contrast, the Japanese regulations on exhaust emissions, the most stringent in the world, set off a wave of innovation which struck terror into the European automobile industry as well. Whereas makers in Europe were laboriously adapting to the use of catalytic converters for exhausts, Japanese automobile engineers had already come up with an environment-friendly solution which does not need a catalyser.[5]

Properly conceived intervention by the state stimulates innovation. It also reduces social costs, thus making the state cheaper. This is my main contention, and it is nowhere better illustrated than by automotive transport.

The example of speed limits provides an especially clear illustration of how cheaply the state can generate (not 'produce') public goods by acting with foresight. A reduction of speeds on highways and motorways would cost the state relatively little for compliance monitoring, but it would have many socially beneficial consequences, for limits on speed reduce:

- the number of accidents,
- the emission of pollutants (nitrogen oxide, carbon monoxide etc.),
- noise pollution,
- energy utilization (at given optimum speeds),
- road surface wear, and
- the need for subsidies for rail travel, as an alternative means of transport.

Much experience and many studies of the reduction in accidents brought about by reduced speed limits are available. An investigation undertaken by

Berlin Technical University, collating a number of different research find-ings, gives the reduction in fatal accidents as follows: 15–25 per cent reduction at 80 km/h on main roads and 30–45 per cent reduction at 100 km/h on motorways.[6] Restricting speed to 30 km/h in built-up areas yields the largest reduction in road traffic fatalities, and also of serious injuries.

The West German Federal Office of the Environment has stated that restricting speeds to 80–100 km/h produces a 19 per cent reduction in nitrogen oxide emission. The Technical University study in question suggested that a 25 per cent reduction could be achieved if engine ratings were suitably adapted.[7] The automobile industry and the Technical Standards Association arrived at lower figures, although the latter assumed, *inter alia*, a low degree of compliance and considered only the Autobahns. These two studies were com-missioned by bodies opposed to the introduction of speed limits and constitute a prime example of science in the service of vested interests.[8]

One of the commissioning bodies was the government of West Germany, a country without speed limits on Autobahns. On this point its capacity for cost-efficient preventive action is clearly less than that of the government of any other developed industrial country. Nevertheless, during the 1960s and 1970s Federal Transport Ministers Seebohm and Lauritzen did make some attempts on their own initiative to curb speeds on motorways and highways, but they were foiled by the car lobby. The present Minister of Transport has been of the opposite persuasion throughout – and has remained a 'successful politician'.

Since we are here citing examples, the example of Japan shows once again that parliamentary governments do have some room for manoeuvre. There the *local* traffic safety committees that were formed in the early 1970s succeeded in strengthening still further the already severe restrictions on maximum speeds on the great majority of motorways and highways. In built-up areas on other than main roads, speeds are generally restricted to 30 or even 20 km/h. Here, as in Japan's policy on clean air, the combination of strict nationwide regula-tions with local freedom to tighten preventive measures has proved conducive to the public good. Furthermore, the number of private vehicles per 1,000 inhabitants in Japan, exporter-in-chief of cars, is little more than half as high as in West Germany, added to which rail travel is nearly always faster there – a decisive advantage where transport is concerned.

If the state takes no action, however, social problems ensue which result in a frenzy of symptom-combating measures. It is expensive to 'deal with' accident prevention by building new roads. In defiance of all views to the contrary, the West German 'long distance road extension law' of 1986 decreed that the Autobahns should be extended from their 1984 length of 8,080 km to 10,450 km. The plan also provides for an additional 3,000 km of highways, and this in a country which already has an extremely high road density.[10] This infrastructure work has made little difference to the toll of accidents. True, road fatalities have fallen, but this is largely due to the compulsory wearing of seat belts, a 'restriction of freedom' which was imposed on motorists.

Another costly element in this transport policy is the insurance cover owing to the increasing number of accidents involving material damage. Equally it is costly when the state proceeds to finance retrofitted catalytic converters instead of insisting upon lean burn energy-saving engines. If ecological modernization of transport were to be adopted, the emphasis would be shifted from nuisance abatement to technical innovation.

Instead, there was actually a slight increase in energy consumption by passenger vehicles per passenger kilometre up to 1983.[11] One of the reasons for this is a growing tendency to over-engine passenger cars, giving them larger engines and so diminishing the effects of more economical performance. To increase horsepower instead of developing economical engines with low toxic exhaust emissions is a technological trend more appropriate to the 1960s; it runs counter to the findings of energy policy for the 1980s.

Energy policy

The impotence of Leviathan can be studied equally well in connection with the electricity supply enterprises. This industry exhibits vested interests similar to those of the automobile industry – not only in West Germany, which is taken here as an example.

- Together with road traffic the electricity supply companies are the most prolific polluters of the air. Yet in many industrial countries they remained almost untouched by the environmental policy of the 1970s. Whilst private householders were reducing their emissions of nitrogen oxide and sulphur dioxide, power stations continued to pour out more of these noxious substances.
- Electricity producers, like road traffic, were but little affected by the energy-saving policy. Whereas the use of primary energy decreased everywhere after the oil crisis, they went on increasing their consumption.[12] The state energetically promoted the use of coal and nuclear energy.
- The industry receives special treatment with regard to taxes and subsidies (see p. 79ff).
- Until well into the 1980s new power stations were being built for which there was no demonstrable need – and this with the support of state energy policy and the building planning authorities, and not infrequently under police protection.
- The electricity supply industry was also assisted by the inflexibility with

which, until well into the 1980s, government departments accepted the unrealistic 'forecasts of requirements' of the industry and gave them legal force in energy policy. The 1973 energy programme of the West German federal government provided for some 60 per cent more primary energy capacity by 1985 than actually proved to be needed. Even in the third statistical update of this programme, published in 1981, the predicted growth rates were only slightly revised downwards.[13]

- Even with respect to 'mobilization potential', the ability to exert political pressure, power producers come a very good second to the automobile industry. Whilst the automobile industry played upon the 'loss of freedom' imposed upon drivers (with votes), the power producers painted lurid pictures of the lights going out. Even the trades unions were brought into these campaigns, to say nothing of political backers.
- Fast breeder reactors illustrate well the high cost of vested interests of this industry. In the 1950s, fast breeder reactors involved a leading edge technology. Yet three decades later, billions of marks are being demanded for it – in the name of 'promoting leading edge technologies' – and so about 7,000 million DM will be dissipated on the fast breeder reactor in Kalkar which is incontestably outdated, will never reach financial break-even point and furthermore involves extreme ecological risks.[14]

Few industries have managed so successfully to enlist the state in the service of their own special interests as has the electricity industry. Therefore it is of particular interest for our purposes.

Even in the very cold January of 1985, when for a time unusually large amounts of current were used, less than 70 per cent of the installed capacity was employed.[15] This amount of overcapacity does not come cheaply, yet the duty of the state, enjoined by the Energy Industry Law, is to make provision for 'cheap' supplies of energy.

The really surprising thing about the ability of the electricity supply companies to achieve such an unchallenged position is that they appear to be particularly well suited as vehicles for the state to use in taking socially beneficial action. First, in West Germany most of them are publicly owned. Second, under the Energy Industry Law they are subject to additional supervision by the state, from planning law to state supervision of pricing. Third, electricity undertakings have to involve the trades unions – which are relatively strongly represented – on their supervisory boards. So how is it that the ability of the state to direct, measured by criteria of public welfare or of environmental prevention, has proved to be so small?

We have here an extreme example of the extent to which, in terms of the theory formulated earlier, a supervisory relationship can be transformed into a sponsoring relationship. In many instances both the representatives of the state and those of the trade unions on the supervisory boards of the power supply undertakings have become the most ardent promoters of the interests of those very undertakings. The monitors have become lobbyists.

This reversal of a supervisory relationship is primarily due to the close relationship engendered on both sides by the very task of monitoring in which they are engaged. Obviously this relationship grows in step with the size and complexity of the entity being monitored, but it is mainly the consequence of the disparate intensities of the monitoring interests on the one hand and the material interest of the monitored object on the other.

What resources has a politician executing a state policy to fall back on when faced with the powerfully organized interests of energy producers? Here again we encounter the loneliness of the representative of the public interest in the state when he comes up against special interests represented massively on a full-time career basis in the shape of corporations and associations. The very need of the politician for information makes him dependent upon the entity he is supposed to be controlling.

The weakness of the state vis-à-vis the electricity industry in Hamburg cost a head of government (Klose) his post, and it finds expression in a variety of other ways. The saga of the breeder reactor is another example (see p. 59). The giant electricity concern RWE, the largest producer of electricity in West Germany, also furnishes a wealth of illustration.[16] I should like to choose another example of which I have personal practical experience – the West Berlin electricity supply undertaking BEWAG. Even the concession agreement made by Land Berlin (West) with BEWAG is a telling illustration of state impotence. This agreement between the government and an undertaking which it owns reads as if it were an agreement to muzzle the state. As such, it is perhaps an extreme example of the role of the state in the energy field. But the fact that in many regions of the Federal Republic concession agreements are guarded like state secrets warrants the conclusion that the situation is not wholly different elsewhere, e.g. where RWE is concerned. In its 1977 version the concession agreement with BEWAG grants that organization extensive rights as sole producer of electricity in Land Berlin (West). In return a licence fee is agreed which remains largely constant over time, and hence falls in relative terms as current consumption rises. That is not all. 'Municipal taxes and other dues to the city introduced since 1 July 1937 levied on the Company in its capacity as a public utility will be deducted from the licence fee payable to the City or, if greater than the amount of the fee, will be credited against future fee payments.' The City furthermore undertakes 'not to levy taxes or other dues on the production, sale or use of electricity or heat'. City administrations have to process applications by BEWAG 'without delay, and without influencing the technical configuration of the installations proposed by the Company'. If the City requires changes to be made to BEWAG installations, it

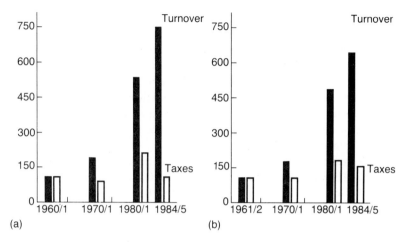

Figure 3 Turnover and taxes of (a) RWE (1960–1 = 100) and (b) BEWAG (1961–2 = 100). *Source*: calculated from the RWE and BEWAG company reports.

must 'reimburse the Company for the costs so occasioned'. The concluding words are: 'If any of these conditions should be invalid in law, the parties undertake as far as possible to replace the invalid condition by one having a similar financial effect.' And this document witnessing to the impotence of a provincial government 'may only be terminated for a serious reason'![17]

What we have here is the agreement between a provincial government and the greatest polluter of its air – and this in an area plagued by smog. With such a power constellation it is not surprising that in the 1970s BEWAG was able to refuse to fit a new power station with flue gas desulphurization equipment that had been specified in the decision approving its construction.

Nor is the scissors graph between payments to the state and the profits and reserves of the electricity producer surprising. Between 1961–2 and 1984–5 BEWAG's free reserves rose from 23 million to 646 million DM, sales of electricity having risen sixfold or sevenfold in the meantime. However, taxes and licence fees did not so much as double, rising from 55 million to 85 million DM.[18]

An even clearer picture emerges with West Germany's largest producer of electricity RWE. Turnover rose between sevenfold and eightfold between 1960–1 and 1984–5. Reserves increased from 339 million to over 3,000 million DM. But the amount of taxes paid remained unchanged, which means that in relative terms they were constantly declining.[19]

In West Berlin the reserves are swollen by another piece of special treatment. There, the investment subsidy is an unusually high one, and it can be encashed twice, once from the Finance Department and again via the electricity tariff. (In reply to a question in parliament it was expressly confirmed in 1982 that 385 million DM had been collected twice in this way for the Reuter West coal-fired power station.)[20] This leads to a frenzied pace of investment and the construction of substantial excess capacity. The constant appearance of new power stations has done more than arouse the anger of the citizens, and West Berlin has the strongest Green–alternative group of any of the provincial parliaments. It has also presented the city with the highest price for electricity in West Germany.[21]

The demeanour of this privileged large industrial concern towards the city is witnessed by the complaint of the Berlin Price Office about what it calls 'the BEWAG colossus': 'Experience so far shows that BEWAG was not prepared to comply with our wishes as regards additional documentation and specifications.' The price monitoring body directs a somewhat forlorn appeal to the Berlin Senate, saying that the Berlin electricity supply undertaking should submit 'convincing supporting documentation' with its accounts.[22]

In 1983 the conduct of BEWAG towards the provincial parliament led to a fracas during a parliamentary hearing when the representative of the power supply undertaking laid the blame for BEWAG's own planning mistakes on the government representatives, because the plans had been approved by the state. The matter under discussion was the Reuter West power station referred to above, which BEWAG had persistently sought permission to build. A version twice the size – 1,200 MW – had been rejected by the courts, and now it was admitted that even the smaller version was overdimensioned. A member of the board announced to the dumfounded MPs that 'of course we can no longer abide by this planning'. Without further ceremony responsibility for the power station under construction in the city centre was shifted onto the state. The project had been 'planning and ideas of the state . . . we would have planned differently if we had been given firm information (in 1980) that such a small rise in power consumption would be involved.'[23] These were the words of one of those who, at the end of the 1970s, foresaw 'the lights going out' unless a power station twice as large was built!

This is a striking example of how at times politics is made the scapegoat even by those who profit from it. One of my reasons for citing this case is to quote the words of a member of parliament whose party (the German Social Democratic Policy) lost its majority in the parliament largely on account of this controversial power station: 'I have the impression that I approved the construction of Reuter West on very imperfect information.'[24] Research Minister von Bülow made a similar comment regarding the fast breeder reactor at Kalkar, after he had resigned from the government. These two cases of conflict may be particularly extreme examples, but they are not the only ones. In the case of the Buschhaus lignite power station the entire Federal Parliament committed itself, and then had to sacrifice its environment-friendly suffrage to the so-called 'realities of the situation'.

It therefore appears that the electricity industry enjoys this quasi-feudal position of strength precisely because of its closeness to the state. But its close links with the machinery of government (or with sections of the trade unions) are only part of the picture. There is also its monopoly position.[25] Instead of the market, the interlocutors are only a few officials in the Price Control Office whose opposition – if it ever comes to that – can easily be disregarded.

Also important is the fact that these entities are joint-stock companies. In West Germany this gives the boards of the electricity supply undertakings a high degree of immunity against the majority shareholder, especially a majority shareholder holding less than 75 per cent of the shares. (Because of this, full public ownership would be an advantage, provided that it was effected at municipal level.[26])

Electricity supply undertakings are now investing thousands of millions in environmental protection. Does that fact invalidate the foregoing analysis? By no means. Because electricity consumption has been rising only slowly since the late 1970s, there is no case for building more power stations. Hence the tendency of this industry to overinvest has opened up a new field of activity, fuelled by increasing public pressure and financed by higher prices for electricity and by subsides. Moreover, the fact that coal production thus becomes relatively dearer gives satisfaction to the nuclear power industry in particular.

Because they made a late start with environmental protection, electricity companies in many EEC countries were behindhand with the technology. So they have had to study desulphurization and denitrogenization techniques in Japan, which had long since developed an export trade in them.

They have also done comparatively little in the way of promoting decentralized and alternative energy production plants. In the 1970s, there was an uncommonly stubborn emphasis on pushing ahead with the development of nuclear energy, and alternative energy sources such as wind energy (in the shape of the German GROWIAN large-scale installation) were absolutely 'researched to death'. Meanwhile alternative energy technologies were being developed into successful export products in Denmark, so much so that by 1984 production was valued at 540 million DM.

Furthermore, many of Denmark's wind power installations are exported to the United States, where in 1984 785 small power plants with a total electricity production capacity of 14,000 MW were planned, capable of supplying 4 million households. Whilst very many nuclear projects were halted, the Americans began to concentrate on alternative renewable energy sources such as the sun, wind or biomass.[27] One of the main foci of these trends was in California, where in 1987 alone windpower with a total output of 1,435 MW was in operation.

Bonn's response to the challenges of the 1970s was not highly rated in a comparative study of the energy policies of France, West Germany, the United States and Sweden. After the United States, Sweden is singled out for special praise, being said to employ 'cooperative and in some cases even plebiscitary methods of resolving political conflicts, which were more supportive of the formation of new interests in energy policy . . . and of their integration into the political decision-making process than in the other . . . countries'.[28] As is known, Sweden had carried out a referendum on nuclear energy in 1980 which resulted in a planned withdrawal from that form of energy. In 1981 the parliament passed laws providing for an energy-saving policy in accordance with the result and a concentrated effort to promote alternative energy sources.

However according to OECD criteria Denmark's energy policy has achieved the greatest success with economy measures which between 1973 and 1983 brought about an appreciable fall in the use of primary energy in absolute terms. Like Norway and Austria, Denmark has renounced the use of nuclear energy, a decision which has not prevented the country from having very low electricity prices.

According to a wide-ranging study of energy published in 1988, energy consumption per head of the population can be halved in the industrial countries by the year 2020 if savings techniques already available are systematically applied, without affecting the level of comfort or inhibiting economic improvement.[29] The problem confronting ecological modernization is not the technologies, and certainly not their economic efficiency. In the West and the East alike, the positions of strength held by the outmoded system of energy supply are the problem.

6 Structural Economic Policy

Not many years ago, aggregates such as the consumption of energy or steel were used as indicators of a country's success. In Eastern Europe a veritable 'tons ideology' was erected on this basis of assessment, but the economies of the West were by no means free from such fetishes. It is no accident that even in 1965 a widely consulted long-term forecast entitled 'formulae for power' erected the consumption of energy and steel into global success indicators, alongside size of population.[1]

Nowadays magnitudes of this sort would more probably be regarded as indicators of failure in the developed economies. In these times of high raw materials costs, increased consumption of energy and materials is seen as uneconomic. The countries that have succeeded in making the largest reductions in specific consumption of materials and energy are now considered the most successful. In the debate on innovation, economy in the use of resources scores high marks. This change of outlook can be highlighted in Robert B. Reich's typological concepts of 'high volume production' as opposed to 'high value production',[2] and it has a basis in environmental policy, namely the simple insight that if less material is used in production, less pollutant is going to be emitted and less waste produced, in addition to the cost savings that would normally result. This is where structural policy comes into play. Structural policy is of considerable importance for environmental and health policy, inasmuch as it concerns the replacement of the old smokestack industries by technology-intensive materials – and energy-saving industries including the services sector, suitable for built-up areas. Such a policy will produce incidental benefits as described earlier, in improved protection of the environment and health.

However, structural policy has also acquired significance for the overall development of the economy and policy. The question whether a structural change will take place in industry and, if so, whether it will come about as a result of crises or because the state takes an active role has become a cardinal question for the economy in many countries.

In several countries an active role for the state would be opposed by advocates of a market economy, sceptical about the state's ability to anticipate the needed developments. The numerous incorrect forecasts relating to energy, transport or finance seem fully to warrant such a liberal *laissez-faire* position, but this overlooks the extent to which such forecasts have in the past been distorted by vested interests rather than inherently mistaken. Moreover, the advantage of a structural policy pursued by the state consists less in the provision of ideal conditions for production than in the avoidance of *foreseeable* crisis situations.

I should like first to illustrate this with an example taken from West Germany, and then to consider the international significance of structural change and the part the state can play in it. The really remarkable thing about the economic scene in West Germany during the 1970s was that there was no lack of pertinent proposals for overcoming the depression. These were concepts of a socially assisted structural reorientation towards products and production methods better adapted to the future. To a considerable extent these proposals were identical with what, ten years later, had become accepted doctrine, and there is no doubt that they would have helped to mitigate the depression. However, they could not prevail against the positions of strength and vested interests built up by the former success industries of the immediate post-war era. What we have in mind are concepts of an 'anticipatory structural policy' marked by ideas of 'qualitative growth' and 'innovative research' (G. Mensch) – concepts which took into account the discussions about energy and the environment then current and which drew inspiration from programmes of that type in Sweden and, above all, Japan.

Typical of this approach was the book *Modernisierung der Volkswirtschaft* (Modernizing the Economy) which appeared in 1975 and was written by Volker Hauff, at that time a secretary of state in Bonn, and Fritz Scharpf, Director of the Berlin Scientific Centre.[3] This was not a socialist or ecological manifesto, but it did reflect the latest findings of enlightened technocrats. It called for changes such as the following:

1 'Every structural concept for industry in the Federal German Republic must be targeted at . . . reducing the international dependence of the German economy as regards energy and raw materials and at the development of new technologies for the recycling of scarce resources. Specifically this means that wasteful production methods must be discouraged or made more expensive and the demand for energy-and raw-material-saving technologies strengthened.'
2 The raw material that West Germany could most usefully increase is the intelligence of its citizens.

3 In future, private and public services should be incorporated into the active structural concept for industry more than has been the case hitherto.

4 'Protection of the environment and the ordered use of space must be two important components of a new structural concept for industry. The demand for environment-friendly technologies . . . is increasing, giving rise to a new market, for which German industry with its special capabilities is particularly well suited.'

5 'Small and medium-sized firms have to take on an important role in a new structural concept for industry.'

This planning concept also included a kind of consensual principle:

We are convinced that even analyses and concepts that are much more soundly based and scientifically backed will have no effect whatever on the real situation of our structural policy until coordination between state and private agents in the process, and the consent of those affected, can be secured through political consensus-building processes in open dialogue. There are so many constraints on the capacity of our political system for manoeuvre . . . that unless consensus is arrived at, an active structural policy having change as its objective is destined to remain an illusion.[4]

A year later, in 1976, a 'Committee for economic and social change in the Federal Republic' that had been set up by the Federal government presented its report, which contained similar calls for structural change. Like Hauff and Scharpf, the report called strongly for comprehensive promotion of innovation with a view to more appropriate 'technology of the future', and for each industry to make the necessary structural changes. It is noteworthy that this report contains many proposals on structural and technology policy which had to wait until the 1980s before they were treated as political novelties – from risk financing to market introduction assistance and the promotion of innovation in small and medium-sized businesses.[5]

The main point of convergence in all these concepts was the demand that the state should transform its 'maintenance subsidies' for structurally weak industries into aids to adaptation and a change of direction. In principle it was not even a request for extra resources, but simply a call for an end to the disastrous policy of high spending on the preservation of outmoded industries, as it was apparent that such activities as mining, heavy industry or construction could not in the long run be artificially sustained at an excessive level of activity. Gerhard Mensch had already written in 1975: 'The depression cannot be cured with the panacea of investment in the construction industry'.[6] He and others wanted instead to see the promotion of timely preparations for new workplaces in the future-oriented industries, and appropriate stimulation of the process of technical and social innovation in the economy.

In 1976 the Bonn Chancellery, after a brief flirtation with the idea, dismissed it as an 'illusion'. This opinion was shared by the Chancellor (who was not overenamoured of his planning department, inherited from Willy Brandt, and preferred to listen to the advice of the chairman of the Mining and Energy trade union).

So what happened? How did West Germany perform in the 1970s? Have events proved the advocates of traditional *laissez-faire* or the advocates of a policy of structural forward planning to be right? There can be little doubt about the answer.

At the Berlin Free University we have been investigating structural change since 1970 in 31 industrial countries to see the environmental impact of changes in the structure of production, measured by material indicators such as energy and steel consumption or the weight of goods transported by rail and road.[7]

It immediately became apparent that a large group of industrial countries has made very little, if any, structural change towards energy-and materials-saving methods of production. This group, which has carried on with the old industrialism more or less unchanged, comprises the countries of Eastern and Southern Europe. (East Germany and Italy were partial exceptions in their respective groups.) This group has not only suffered worsening environmental problems; it has also experienced considerable economic problems in the shape of high costs and an absence of innovation. Most of the members of this group with a capitalist economic system showed a strong tendency to experience large-scale unemployment.

Table 5 shows some countries with particularly marked structural change. Here also there are two variants. In some of those countries employment actually increased after the oil crisis, or (as in Denmark) at least remained at a high level, whereas in others, where marked structural change occurred, employment fell (it should be remembered that the level of employment is a better standard of comparison than the figures for unemployment). The less successful group includes Belgium, West Germany and the United Kingdom, countries which reacted to the challenge of high raw materials prices with a mixture of structure conservatism and *laissez-faire*. At the same time these are countries which, like Japan or some of the countries in Eastern Europe, suffered from 'overindustrialization' in the form of hypertrophied basic industries.

Japan is one of the countries in which structural change was accompanied by a more successful employment policy, even though there the ecological advantage of a decrease in energy consumption or freight carried was largely neutralized by the rapid growth of the economy. In Japan the state not only

Table 5 Employment, structural change and economic performance in Western industrial countries 1973–83 (percentage changes)

Country	Employment		Structural change				Economic performance in terms of GNP (real)
	Employees per 100 people aged between 15–64 years and (1983)	Civil employment	Primary energy consumption	Raw steel consumption	Goods transport weight[a]		
Structural change with rising/sustained high employment							
Sweden	78.5	+ 8.9	+ 2.5	–40.8	–29.1		+ 14.6
Denmark	71.7	0.0	–15.0	–43.7	+ 5.5		+ 18.3
Japan	71.1	+ 9.0	+ 2.2	–31.6	+ 2.0		+ 41.4
USA	65.9	+ 18.5	–2.3	–36.8			+ 22.7
Structural change with a decrease in employment							
Great Britain	64.7	–6.0	–12.9	–43.1	–17.3		+ 8.8
West Germany	59.9	–6.7	–5.4	–26.2	–9.2		+ 18.3
Belgium/Luxemburg	55.5[b]	–4.3	–16.6	–31.2[c]	+ 0.6		+ 14.7

[a]Rail and road transport.
[b]Belgium only.
[c]1973–81.

took timely action to develop initiatives on environmental and energy policies; it also intervened actively to promote the structural transformation of production from extensive to intensive methods, with aids to reorganization and redirection of effort. Declining industries were assisted to close down unwanted capacity quickly and encouraged to reassign capital and labour for the future. In addition to medium-term forward planning there were redirective concepts such as the 'Plan for an Information Society' issued in 1972, or the 'Sunshine Programme' for energy saving.

An essential feature of policy on employment was that productivity increases were consciously geared not only to the 'labour factor' but quite deliberately to materials consumption and energy as well. For example, between 1975 and 1979 the steel industry increased its productivity more through materials saving than through labour shedding by rationalization. In the automobile industry savings on labour and materials contributed about equally to the increase in productivity.[8]

Next to Japan, all five of the Nordic countries came through the structural crisis with the highest level of employment among Western countries. Moreover all of them except Denmark recorded an increase in employment. Norway had a specially impressive 18.3 per cent increase, although owing to its oil boom the country did not undergo such far-reaching structural changes.

Sweden is particularly interesting in this respect. There the indicators of heavy traditional smokestack industry fell in absolute terms to an extent that must be classed as a noteworthy gratis effect of environmental protection. Indicators ranging from steel to cement changed drastically, whilst the weight of goods transported fell by nearly a third between 1973 and 1983.

Measured by such 'quantitative indicators', Sweden had the greatest incubus of heavy traditional industrial production among 31 industrial countries in 1970. It was therefore not surprising that in 1969 Sweden became the first European country to see the need for a comprehensive policy of environmental protection, and by 1980 the picture had changed radically, more so than in any other industrial country.[9]

The numbers employed in industry fell by 15 per cent between 1975 and 1983, yet this was accompanied by a substantial rise in the numbers of gainfully occupied persons. Sweden has the highest level of employment among Western countries. This owes much to early specialization in knowledge-intensive technologies and in services with export potential, but municipal services were also considerably expanded.

It should be noted that Sweden had to incur massive debts in order to fund the success story. Nevertheless, we see here the effects of a forward-looking structural and technological policy with particular stress on environmental and energy policy. This was achieved in the context of a consensual approach and may well have been helped by the codetermination arrangements prevailing in industry and commerce.

Denmark presents a similar picture in many respects, although unemployment is higher. As mentioned previously, the country has done particularly well in energy policy. Between 1973 and 1983 Denmark achieved considerable savings, and not only through the decline of energy-intensive branches of industry, i.e. through the mechanism of crisis. In this respect, alternative environment-friendly energy techniques, as well as municipal techniques, have been developed into successful export products. Like Sweden, Denmark now has a high proportion of 'tertiary' economic activities. Furthermore, agriculture has retained its important place in the overall economy. The level of agricultural employment is higher than in West Germany, and the workforce includes large numbers of women. Notwithstanding the far-reaching structural changes in the macroeconomy, Sweden and Denmark are two of the richest countries in Europe.

. In terms of the absolute decline of the traditional 'quantitative' indicators previously mentioned, the United Kingdom and Belgium too had effected a radical structural change, but it was not achieved by the state, using assistance measures to promote restructuring. It was brought about mainly by crises postponed, yet not in the end avoided, by state action.

West Germany too provides an example of the steering effect of the crisis mechanism. Crises were wholly responsible for bringing about structural change in the sense of the decline of the old smokestack industries, the construction industry etc. In that process the destructive aspect of the crisis mechanism took full effect, but its constructive side did not. The market provided insufficient new openings. Such failure generally triggers action by the state in the field of structural policy. According to Guy Kirsch this entails a risk that the state will 'degenerate into a feudalistic mould, becoming a guarantor of the inflexibility which it ought to be trying to combat'.[10] The experience of Scandinavia and Japan shows that this is not inevitable; nevertheless it did happen in the case of West Germany and other EEC countries.

In 1974 I took part in a planning discussion in Bonn at which there was a strong disposition to allow the construction industry to shrink to its natural dimensions. In the same year, which was marked by a severe recession, the first programme to be approved included assistance for the construction industry. Over the next few years this was followed by a whole series of similar costly programmes in rapid succession.[11] It is true that these programmes contained an element of modernization, such as the construction of sewage treatment works, domestic heat insulation and inner city renewal, but their main characteristic was a refusal to contemplate ending the growth of such an important industry as construction, or to relinquish this 'engine of growth'.

After 1973 an increasing number of industries began to receive state assistance of the most varied kinds, nearly all of which ran counter to the principle laid down officially by the government in 1968 that 'Aid must in no case serve to maintain the status quo; instead it must promote restructuring and "self-help".'[12]

These measures created very few jobs, and certainly no permanent ones. On the contrary, the West German state did its best to promote job losses. Investment assistance was heavily biased in that direction. Productivity was increased by economizing on labour rather than on resource utilization, so that the aid given to the old industries preserved their structure whilst tending to accelerate labour shedding.

A reactive structural policy like this may well have more deleterious effects than no structural policy at all, since it hinders rather than encourages the process of change. Because of this, international comparisons show that even countries with a pronounced market economy philosophy have coped with structural change more successfully. For example, in the United States the services sector created 22.4 million new jobs between 1970 and 1984 whereas the industrial sector, so strongly encouraged in every respect, did not create any new opening for gainful employment.[13]

Conservatives always cite the American 'employment miracle' as a standard argument of their market philosophy, whilst saying nothing about similar successes in Sweden and, above all, Norway, but it should be pointed out that unemployment has remained higher in the United States than in these two countries. The level of employment, too, is lower than in Scandinavia or Japan. Where the market has effected the structural changes it has plunged whole regions into depression with very little cushioning by the state, resulting in severe impoverishment. Yet it would be a serious mistake to ignore the United States as having nothing to teach those engaged in the search for better solutions. Markets have a significantly lower failure rate when new economies have to be created. A tradition of simplicity in the formation of new enterprises is always an advantage in times of change. Moreover, state intervention is by no means unknown in the United States. Until 1980 the state played a more active role there in energy and environmental policy than in most EEC countries. At individual state level, structural economic policy appears to be anything but a no-go area.

Thus the international picture of successes and failures in structural change is a picture of great variety. Failures by both states and markets are important in this respect.

I began this description of state failure with health services. This sector swallows up enormous sums comparable with those absorbed by economic intervention aimed at perpetuating the status quo. Both these areas exhibit striking structural deficiencies – deficiencies which in my judgement have a great deal in common.

Whereas in the health field public goods of low quality are being sold at ever-increasing prices, in other areas of policy they come largely free of charge, as a side effect. This also applies to other in-depth forms of preventive medicine such as protection of the environment, the preventive variants of which again relate to areas such as policy on energy and transport. The ecological modernization of these areas is supplemented by technical and structural change in production methods and facilities.

In other words, a society which invests in an ecologically and socially appropriate production structure is supplying public goods free of charge as gratis effects in other areas of policy. Consequently there is something to be said for redeploying funds from *post facto* remedial action (nuisance abatement) and concentrating on the beneficial effects of structural change. There are, besides, economic reasons of considerable weight.

But in fact even the structural change in the manufacturing sector has been to a large extent a gratis effect. In most of the industrial countries it had little to do with considerations of environmental, health or energy policy. It was first and foremost a reaction to spiralling costs, especially severe with regard to oil prices but by no means confined to them.

It is almost incredible that the same redirective effect as was produced by a price crisis could have been brought about by selective taxation to promote restructuring, and it says much about the world economy and the role of the state therein that a virtual 'tax' suddenly and unilaterally placed on oil by the Organization of Petroleum Exporting Countries (OPEC) was taken on board, whilst even a fraction of these additional charges in the form of payments to the state would have had business and industry in the industrial countries up in arms.

In a period of falling raw materials prices this is precisely the lesson that has to be learned, however. Price mechanisms do indeed have an important guidance function, and taxation by the state can and must make use of it. Taxes on energy and raw materials, which have long been called for, are a useful instrument for this purpose. A computer calculation carried out at Berlin Technical University indicates that this instrument would be likely to produce considerable effects on employment, savings and innovation.[14]

If all the desiderata discussed in this chapter are left entirely to the market, state failure will have occurred.

7 State Failure as State Indebtedness

Institutionalized deficits

It might be contended that the increase in public debt is not 'failure by the state', since no 'public good' is being produced. But this borderline case of the non-production of a good at constantly increasing cost – interests – is just what makes the subject so explosive. In many Western countries interest payments have become one of the most considerable items in the budget. In West Germany they had already reached the same order of magnitude as the defence budget by 1984. In the same year 5 per cent of the national annual economic outturn had to be paid in government interest in the United States, and as much as 10 per cent in Italy. Even more alarming is the *trend* of the interest burden. Whereas in 1970 only 2.8 per cent of West Germany's federal budget was spent on interest, by 1980 this had increased to 6.5 per cent. And by 1992, according to the finance planners, it will amount to nearly 13 per cent![1]

Thus the public good sold in this way at such a high, and increasing, price is not merely deficient in quality as, say, inadequate protection of the environment would be. It has no quality at all, because no such 'good' exists. Yet enormous incomes are earned from this state non-activity. By far the greater part of this budgetary item in West Germany is paid to the banks and savings institutions,[2] which also do profitable business with government loans. The following message appeared in the *Wirtschaftswoche* (24 May 1985) in a report on the Bayerische Landesbank Girozentrale: 'The second largest provincial bank in Germany does 40 per cent of its business with the public authorities . . . it continues to bank on the preparedness of government establishments to incur debt, and the "very large market" associated with this . . . notwithstanding the trend towards consolidation, an increase in federal and provincial state indebtedness is to be expected.'

Were it not for the growth of the banks at the expense of indebted govern-ments (one of the few growth industries in Western countries), the item for 'interest' in state budgets would presumably come under even closer adverse scrutiny.

It is not simply that debts are incurred and interest paid on them. That is normal and reasonable in any private household or business undertaking. Nor is the problem caused by an increase in indebtedness for investments that will be paid for by an adequate return from taxation. Part of the problem is the 'economic inefficiency' of contracting debts which will not generate any extra dividends – debts which instead of mobilizing future potential simply pay for missed opportunities of the past.

The core of the problem, however, is the inveterate pursuit of such policies by governments even in times of economic prosperity. In many Western countries the trend of state indebtedness only began to rise after 1970 (table 6). In this context a trend means that an unbalanced budget was not caused, as it used to be, by special non-recurrent circumstances, but rather that the deficit was becoming a permanent feature. After ten years the problem had become considerably more acute. In nearly all the Western countries the annual budget deficits were higher than the growth rate of GNP in real terms by the beginning of the 1980s and annual interest payments followed suit – and the irony was that the debts were being incurred with the aim of boosting economic growth.

Nowadays there are substantial deficits even in the 'good' times. In 1986 West Germany had a growth rate of 2.3 per cent in real terms, but even in that year public deficit equal to 1.2 per cent of gross domestic product was incurred. In the United States a growth rate of 2.9 per cent was achieved in 1986, yet still the additional public deficit amounted to 3.4 per cent of gross domestic product. The position is substantially less favourable in Italy, Belgium and Ireland.

Now 'economic upswings' do not lead to repayment of the indebtedness. Indeed, they are to a very large extent the result of deficit financing. This is how an illusion of growth arises, masking the persistence of the structural crisis. During the 1980s most of the Western industrial countries would have had distinctly lower growth rates but for public sector borrowing; indeed in some cases only credit-financed demand prevented the appearance of negative growth rates. Taking the first half of the 1980s as a whole, state indebtedness masks economic stagnation in most Western countries, with Finland and Norway among the exceptions.[3]

This means that in contrast with the 1970s there are few or no reserves avail-able for the bad times – for a downturn in the economy. What would happen if the overindebted world economy plunged into recession as it did 60 years ago?

Table 6   Expenditure, deficits and interest of the state sector as a percentage of gross domestic product 1970–84

		West Germany	France	Italy	Japan	USA	UK
Total expenditure	1970	39.0	39.3	34.7	19.3	32.9	39.7
	1975	48.7	43.9	43.4	27.3	36.0	46.4
	1980	47.5	46.7	46.3	32.2	35.3	43.9
	1984	47.4	52.3	59.2	34.2	36.9	46.4
Financial surplus	1970	0.2	0.9	–3.5	1.8	–1.4	2.5
or deficit (–)	1975	–5.7	–2.2	–11.7	–2.8	–4.3	–4.7
	1980	–3.2	0.2	–8.0	–3.9	–1.0	–3.7
	1984	–2.3	–3.0	–13.6	–2.7	–3.4	–3.6
Interest payments	1970	0.9	1.1	1.8	0.6	2.3	3.9
	1975	1.3	1.3	4.0	1.2	2.5	4.0
	1980	1.9	1.6	6.3	3.2	3.3	5.0
	1984	2.9	2.9	9.7	3.9[a]	5.1	5.1

[a]Figures for 1982.
Source: DIW Weekly Report, 24, 1985.

Medium-term financial planning for the coming years bears the strong imprint of the propensity of states to contract debts almost as a matter of routine. Although the starting assumption is a relatively favourable economic trend, it is planned to contract a considerable amount of new debt. Even with a spartan regime of economy, Belgium was hoping to reduce its budget deficit from 12.8 per cent of gross domestic product in 1983 to 'only' 7 per cent in 1987.[4] Other EEC countries are in a similar position.[5] Overall the EEC expects its members to have an annual deficit amounting to 4 per cent of gross domestic product by 1990 – and this on the favourable assumptions of an 'optimistic' scenario.[6]

West Germany is in the less heavily committed half of the Western industrial countries as regards contracting public debt, but even there the ambition of the Finance Minister, applauded by other nations, is to reduce the federal deficits to 'only' about 30,000 million DM by 1992. On top of this come the new loans contracted by the regional states and the local authorities in West Germany.[7] The medium-term financial plan is predicated on continuing economic expansion. A computer simulation carried out by the federal government forecasts a deficit of all public authority budgets amounting to 17,000 million DM even in 1995 – provided that all goes well.[8]

The total of central, regional and local government debt in West Germany, which amounted to 843,000 million DM in 1987[9], will in any event increase still further, automatically raising interest payments. Amortization payments will also rise still further in the next few years. The federal government alone had to find 55,900 million DM for this purpose in 1987, compared with 43,500 million DM in 1984.[10]

In the United States the federal government, at least, will also continue contracting new debt until 1993, even on the most favourable forecasts. The optimistic assumptions of the government, which predict an improvement thereafter, are predicated on strong growth of the economy, a fall in unemployment and decreasing inflation.[11] The combination of *laissez-faire* strategy and massive rearmament has not been good for the American federal budget, and it has been worse for the world economy. The fact that the indebtedness of the United States is of average proportions internationally is a comment on the international position, but the problem is rendered critical for the United States by heavy indebtedness permeating the economy, from foreign trade to the consumers,[12] for this creates a dangerous dependence on monetary inflows from abroad. And the fate of the world economy really depends on the question whether the hegemonial power of the America will secure these financial flows.

By 1990 budgetary deficits will be an institution of two decades' standing in most of the industrial countries of the West. At the beginning of the 1970s the alarmed advocates of saving on all sides were still cherishing the aim of demolishing the mountain of debt that had arisen, but in the 1980s the situation has changed. The aim is no longer to reduce the mountain of debt, but only to contract less new indebtedness. It is limited to slowing the pace at which nations go more deeply into debt. This contraction of the horizon of aims is a sign that states are becoming less able to influence developments. It is a pointer to the political impotence of the state and in the state.

Causes of indebtedness since 1970: does the welfare state cost too much?

What has caused the expenditure and income lines of public finance to scissor? The answer must be sought first in expenditure, which rose persistently in the 1970s.

At first sight it is comparatively easy to identify the causes of the expansion in government expenditures since 1970. The OECD has compared the government expenditures of nine leading Western countries, including the United Kingdom, West Germany, the United States and Japan, for 1970 and 1981. For the sake of comparability these expenditures have been expressed as a proportion of gross domestic product (which is mostly the same as GNP). These data enable the causes of the increase in state expenditure in the nine countries to be ranked as follows.

1 Pensions: expenditure on these averaged 2.7 percentage points of gross domestic product higher than in 1970, bringing it to 9.1 per cent of GDP.
2 Interest on government debt: this rose by 2 percentage points of gross domestic product.
3 Subsidies: these rose by an average of 1.3 percentage points of GDP. (This datum included 21 Western countries over the period 1970–82.)
4 Health and on statutory health insurance: state expenditure on this rose by 1.2 percentage points during the 11-year period.
5 Unemployment: government expenditure on unemployment rose by 1 percentage point of GDP.
6 Education: state expenditure on this increased by 0.8 per cent of gross domestic product.
7 Housing and local services: state expenditure on this has increased by 0.5 percentage points.

The seven items listed make up an increase of nearly 10 per cent of GDP. (The fact that government expenditure in the nine countries rose by less than this proportion during the eleven years is due to the relative decrease in some other types of expenditure.)

At first sight this listing would seem to indicate that the welfare state is costing too much. There was a disproportionate increase in pensions and in expenditure on health, education and social benefits. It would appear that the thesis of the 'inflation of citizens' expectations' is confirmed. But a second look reveals a quite different picture.

The increase in the percentage value of pensions payments is quite adequately explained by the further increase in life expectancy of the citizens. Particularly in Japan, the rapid increase in the number of old people has posed problems for the state finances. There is no doubt that the simultaneous decrease in the younger age groups at a time when the population is steadily growing creates a delicate problem of inter-generation redistribution, with which the state has to cope financially, but this is the inevitable consequence of a population trend, and the subject therefore has no place in a critical financial analysis.

Nor are pensions the largest item in the foregoing list, if debt repayment is taken together with interest payments (which are carefully tucked away in the financial statistics). Quite obviously debt servicing is the largest individual item among the disproportionate increases in state expenditure in the industrial countries of the West. These increases are therefore both the consequence and the fomenter of the policy of indebtedness.

Unlike pensions or unemployment benefit, debt servicing payments go to a powerful industry, the financial sector, which in this area is selling its services at the expense of the state. The greater part of the subsidies also go to the private economy, as do most of the remaining increasing expenditures which find their way into the social–industrial complex. This will be explained in more detail later on.

Tax expenditures: overt and covert tax waivers

This is another kind of expenditure, the existence of which is sometimes largely hidden. It concerns what are known as 'tax expenditures': these are waivers of public income, based on special law but excluded from the formal decision-making process on budgets. They are very relevant to our subject, because state indebtedness also has to do with revenue shortfalls.

Adequate information about the international aspect of 'tax expenditures' is not available. In West Germany they amounted to 7.9 per cent of federal revenues in 1980. In the same year they were 3.5 per cent of the national income in Austria.[14] In the United States, 'tax expenditures' are considerably higher than in these two countries. Tax concessions on commercial and household building loans amounted to $182,000 million in the United States in 1986, compared with $117,000 million in 1981.[15] Overall there is not enough reliable data to determine whether 'tax expenditures' form a major part of the growth in deficits in state revenues. However, the picture immediately becomes clearer if we consider the movement of particular types of taxes rather than tax remissions for particular purposes.

In West Germany the following tax receipts have risen by less than the norm since 1970: property tax, income tax, turnover tax on domestic products, tobacco tax, duties on spirits, vehicle tax and petroleum tax; road freight tax, which in 1971 yielded 468 million DM, was even abolished.

Measured by the average movement of tax since 1970, this represents a formidable waiver of tax revenue every year. But that is not all, for there were also revenue waivers of millions of marks in favour of an industry that is as powerful as it is in need of reorientation through taxation – the electricity industry.

We have already touched upon the privileged tax position of this industry. It is remarkable even in comparison with other tax concessions. Whereas tax revenue rose by 172 per cent between 1970 and 1984 (see table 7), taxes paid by RWE rose by only 13.7 per cent in all. BEWAG's tax payments rose by 54.5 per cent, and in both cases taxes formed a correspondingly smaller

Table 7   Index of tax revenues rising at a disproportionately low rate in West Germany, 1970–84

Type of tax	1970	1984
All taxes	100	272
Tobacco tax	100	221
Petroleum tax	100	209
Turnover tax on domestic products	100	207
Spirits duties	100	190
Road vehicle tax	100	190
Assessed income tax	100	165
Property tax	100	156
Road freight tax	100	0[a]
By contrast: Wage tax	100	389

[a]Abolished at the end of 1971.

Source: Federal Republic of Germany Statistical Yearbook, 1972, 1985; own calculations

proportion of turnover. Whereas BEWAG of Berlin paid 16.5 per cent of its sales revenue in taxes and licence fees in 1961–2, by 1970–1 this had fallen to 9.1 per cent and by 1984–5 to a total of 3.9 per cent![17]

This decreasing incidence of tax on the incomes of electricity companies is particularly unjustifiable. Whilst the state was getting ever more deeply into debt, this sector of industry almost completely insulated against depression was stashing away thousands of millions of marks in reserves. When these reserves were liquidated, they were often invested in large unprofitable capital projects, resulting in substantial overcapacities, the costs of which immediately drove up the price of electricity, as the public Price Office is not concerned with profitability, but with proof of higher costs. Moreover, as has already been mentioned, some of these investment costs were accepted even though they were never incurred, because they were refunded by the state. What an encouragement to make uneconomic investments! And what an incentive to impose unjustified price rises!

So if the electricity producers were to pay more taxes in West Germany, it would by no means necessarily lead to higher prices for electricity, even if they were useful in terms of energy policy. The first effect would be to run down the reserves, resulting in a more economic conduct of investment, at least if the government pricing inspectors refused to allow reasonable taxes to be passed on in electricity prices. In the worst case the fat dividends might have to be trimmed; their importance to the state revenues is frequently overestimated. However, this would only reinforce the incentive to make reasonable investments, and the frequently invoked competitiveness of the enterprises would not suffer, for there is no competition.

All in all, the revenue-raising side of the federal finances in West Germany shows evidence of partiality in several directions.

(1) A considerable bias in favour of road transport: this is true of the road vehicle tax, for example. The number of road vehicles has nearly doubled since 1970, and the horsepower and value of automobiles have also increased significantly. So has awareness of the problems they create. A rise of only 90 per cent in tax paid does not give nearly enough weight to this perception. Road freight enjoys even vaster tax concessions. When it was first taxed in 1968 the purpose was avowedly to compensate for the competitive disadvantages of rail freight compared with road freight. Yet at the end of 1971 the road freight tax was abolished.

(2) Petroleum consumption receives favourable treatment, at least if the tax paid is compared with the very rapid increase in turnover. Consumption of gasoline, unlike that of fuel oil, has also greatly increased in volume. Until 1988 gasoline was taxed more lightly in West Germany than in the other EEC countries, with the exception of Luxembourg.[18]

(3) Lenient treatment of alcohol and tobacco consumption: it is true that the small increase in consumption might be held to justify the disproportionately low increase in tax income from these products, but some countries tax them far more heavily for reasons of health policy. Moreover, we shall meet the tobacco industry again when we come to examine subsidies, an area in which it enjoys very favourable treatment.

(4) Electricity consumption is favoured.

(5) The labour factor is greatly disadvantaged.

Besides its other disadvantages, this policy on taxation has tended to increase expenditure. It has done this in at least four respects:

- The revenue shortfalls have driven up the cost of debt servicing which in 1984 had reached the gigantic figure of more than 130,000 million DM![19]
- The very substantial assistance given to road transport has reduced (relatively) the profitability of the railways, increasing their already heavy claim for subsidies.
- The high taxation of wage and salary earners has made labour dearer and increased the incentive to economize on labour, increasing the amount that was paid out in unemployment benefit.
- The gentle treatment of tobacco and alcohol producers and the favourable treatment of electricity producers and road traffic has undoubtedly increased the cost of damage to health and to the environment.

In brief, a more consistent taxation policy would also have contributed to a policy of economy. In the long term it would have created budgetary room for tax reductions.

There can be no doubt at all that there were obvious alternatives in the field of structural policy to the policy of indebtedness with respect to the revenue side alone of the national finances of West Germany. Not only were 'tax expenditures' in the shape of special tax concessions, as already described, incurred; in some cases tax remission involving large amounts of revenue was granted to particular branches of industry – automobiles, drinks and tobacco, energy supply – or to the entire business sector.

As in West Germany, so in other Western countries disproportionate rises in the taxation of wages and salaries go hand in hand with concessions on corporate taxation. In the United States the share of corporate taxes in federal receipts under several governments fell significantly between 1960 and 1985; it may rise slightly again following President Reagan's tax reform.[20] A survey relating to 275 large corporations in the USA shows that a substantial rise is due. During Reagan's first period of office they paid only one-third of the $184,000 million they owed. Fifty of them paid nothing, despite making high profits. And corporations such as Boeing, Dow Chemical and ITT even received tax credits![21]

After this excursus about revenues, let us return to expenditure. We have already seen that debt servicing has been the strongest-growing item of expenditure: it now becomes clear that this strong growth is also a consequence of tax waivers.

This calculation can be done using either a narrow or a broad definition of tax waivers. Whichever is chosen, the potential for budget consolidation is enormous, and it is not the only possible means of correction to be revealed.

Subsidies – a policy harmful to the environment and health

Another way is to look at the expenditure item with the third highest growth rate (after pensions), namely subsidies. In the first place, this item is considerably larger than the official financial statistics show. The Kiel Institute for World Economy has calculated that in 1985 subsidies amounting to 121,500 million DM were paid out in West Germany (table 8), although this does include tax remission amounting to about 30 per cent of the total.

At first sight the largest item of subsidy would suggest the picture of the 'expensive' welfare state, but a further look shows that it covers mainly assistance to the construction industry which state investment policy strongly

Table 8   Subsidies in the Federal Republic of Germany (thousand million DM)

	1973	1980	1985
Agriculture, forestry and fisheries	10.2	16.7	20.0
Industry (excluding construction)	8.5	16.7	20.0
Energy and mining	2.3	7.0	7.1
Iron producing industry, foundries etc.	0.2	0.5	2.0
Construction and housing	10.6	18.2	24.0
Transport and communications	12.4	20.9	23.1
Commerce, banking and other services	5.7	12.9	14.8
Private non-profitmaking organizations (churches, Red Cross etc.)	8.4	15.2	18.9
Total	55.7	100.5	121.5

Source: E. Gerken et al., *Subventionsabbau in der Bundesrepublik Deutschland*, Institut für Weltwirtschaft, October 1985, p. 11; own compilation with rounding differences

encourages in any event. The promotion of housing construction by the state has had deleterious effects on town planning and ecology, and ultimately on social policy as well (because it helped to eliminate cheap living accommodation).

The second largest item consists of aid to two state enterprises, the railways and the post office. These subsidies were needed largely because the two enterprises themselves have to pay covert subsidies in the form of tariff reductions, such as the newspaper postal service. As already noted, the railway subsidies also include avoidable expenses of state promotion of the use of automobiles. This does not mean only the building of public roads or waivers of vehicle and road freight taxes. The state also pays direct subsidies to the automobile industry and to road traffic (see p. 85).

The next largest item of subsidies might at first glance again confirm conservative critics of the welfare state in their views: this is 'help for farmers'. However, closer examination reveals that this too mainly covers transfer payments destined for branches of industry which depend on agriculture, such as agrochemistry, agricultural machinery and wholesale trade etc. These transfer payments arise from the fact that the share of industrial inputs for each agricultural product has steadily risen. If it were primarily a result of the conduct of the welfare state, farmers, and especially small farmers, would be better off than in fact they are. Here too reasons of both social policy and ecology, over and above fiscal considerations, suggest that a radical change would be in order. In particular, the agricultural policy of the EEC has promoted a dubious quantitative growth at the expense of the quality of food and the environment, and the surpluses so produced, which have to be disposed of on the international market for agricultural produce with the aid of yet more subsidies, create competitive difficulties there too for Third World countries, unable to afford such heavy subsidization.

The fourth largest item of subsidies goes to industry. This kind of subsidy too might be justified if it served to promote reorientation and innovation directed towards products and production methods appropriate to the future. But research undertaken by the *Deutsches Institut für Wirtschaftsforschung* (DIW) showed that in 1982 only just 1.5 per cent of the subsidies given by central government were for modernization, in addition to 6.3 per cent for research, development and environmental protection. Thirty-six per cent of all such expenditures served to maintain the status quo. Indeed, this share is in fact considerably greater if the assistance received by the construction industry is also taken into account.[22]

And that is the main problem with this huge financial outlay. It removes the pressure to change from established branches of industry. It promotes structural sclerosis in industry by artificially maintaining products at a higher level than real demand would require. It is either paid to large firms or sectors which have no special need of subsidies, such as banking, insurance, chemicals and electrical engineering, or else it is given to branches of industry which from an ecological and structural policy viewpoint should not receive additional assistance.

Indeed, this state of affairs is so remarkable as to merit special emphasis here. According to the aforementioned DIW study, which concentrates mainly on subsidies paid by central government, between 1970 and 1982 the following groups of industries received subsidies which increased at an above-average rate.

1 The housing–construction–stone industry received 8,900 million DM in 1982 compared with 2,900 million DM in 1970.
2 The energy sector (including petroleum refining) received 6,200 million DM compared with 1,400 million DM in 1970.
3 Road traffic received 1,000 million DM compared with 390 million DM in 1970; the Federal Railways similarly needed a subsidy increased to 9,400 million DM compared with 3,600 million DM in 1970.
4 The iron producing industry, engineering and shipbuilding received 1,900 million DM compared with 678 million DM in 1970.
5 The chemicals industry received 928 million DM compared with 314 million DM in 1970.

6   The tobacco and drinks industry also received a subsidy increase from 221 million in 1970 to 695 million DM in 1982.[23]

Thus at the expense of the taxpayer, or on credit, more open country was built over, more automobile traffic created, more energy and metal used, more smoking and drinking done and more chemical products consumed. If this were all due to a cynical plan (which it was not) we could almost say that the state had done what it could, by providing subsidies, to drive up the costs of environmental and health protection. And these, remember, were only the subsidies that grew by more than the average.

It might be objected that construction subsidies are also good for inner city renewal, and energy subsidies for energy saving. This is true, but it involves only minute shares. For example, whilst comparatively small amounts were spent on energy conservation, huge subsidies were paid to coal and nuclear energy production, and it is hard to discern any rationality in assistance whereby saving *and* squandering, or road *and* rail, are indiscriminately promoted at the same time. The conclusion of the DIW seems incontrovertible: 'Much of the action taken does not serve to achieve defensible goals or else runs counter to other important aims.[24]

Avoidable costs of unemployment

Are not the high and rising costs of unemployment, at least, a price that has to be paid for the economic situation that has developed? With regard to a large part of these costs, I emphatically deny this assertion. In support of my view the example of countries which have had as low an economic growth rate as West Germany and yet were able to achieve almost full employment, including Switzerland, Luxembourg, New Zealand, and Sweden, could be generally cited. I cannot go into further detail here, and shall confine myself to a few general observations.

The unemployment which has occurred is partly the result of failure to give a political lead in the area of active structural and labour market policy. If the huge subsidies had not constituted an investment in conserving the existing structure of industry, but instead had been given for the purpose of reorientation and retraining, then the experience of other countries shows that the employment situation would have been much better.

However, even policy on the labour market was to a large extent a policy of combating symptoms. The funding of active labour market policies has been constantly decreasing as a proportion of overall costs of unemployment ever since 1973, and from 1981 to 1983 it fell in absolute terms.[25] Moreover, mass unemployment and its consequential costs to the state are also a result of the fact that the increase in state expenditure was financed mainly via the 'labour factor' which, not surprisingly, became more expensive in consequence.

Lastly and most importantly, the mass unemployment which has occurred is the result of failure to take steps in connection with employment policy which were being publicly discussed. For example, a substantial effect on employment could have been achieved by a cost-neutral redistribution of state personnel costs. By this I mean savings in the upper income brackets in favour of more posts in the lower income brackets. Another area where energetic action certainly was not, and is not, being taken is the manifold forms of work redistribution. Nor is self-employment by workers operating factories closed by firms being promoted. Furthermore, if new small enterprises were as vigorously promoted as the old large corporations, not only would the economy be better adapted but also more people would be in employment. The alternative enterprises, which created at least 24,000 jobs, suffered downright discrimination, and not only with regard to loans and credit.[26] Nor is this list exhaustive. It is only cited in order to substantiate the claim that the escalation of the costs of unemployment too was – and still is – to a large extent avoidable.

Financial planning: loss of realism at the centres

In addition to the reasons already adduced for the prevalence of budgetary deficits, some of which are already under discussion, there is a set of causes hardly mentioned so far, but which in the overall context of this work is of crucial importance. I refer to functional state failure in financial planning, especially the finances of central governments. What I have in mind can be illustrated by the examples of West Germany, the United States and Sweden.

In all three countries state indebtedness has been primarily an affair of the central government, as it has been in other Western countries as well. In contrast, surpluses have often been achieved at levels below that of central government.

In West Germany the accumulated liabilities of local authorities amount to only one-seventh of total public debt. They have risen only slowly since 1979, and in 1985 these authorities turned in a balanced budget. The central state is responsible for more than half of the mountain of debt.[27]

In the United States central government has an even larger share of the accumulated liabilities, and between 1974 and 1982 this share rose from 70.2 to 74.2 per cent. Here too the local authorities have shown the smallest increase in indebtedness, at least since 1975.[28] In Sweden too it is above all central government which contracted debts during and after the 1970s. By contrast, the municipalities were in a comparatively strong financial position. In 1984, therefore, the Finance Ministry allowed the municipalities a small amount of growth, whilst central state expenditure was supposed to fall in real terms.[29]

What matters is the quality of the financial planning of the central governments. I maintain that a not inconsiderable portion of the indebtedness is due to faulty medium-term planning of the finances. Central planners have an ingrained tendency to overestimate their receipts and to underestimate the expenditures that will be caused by problems. This results in additional loans being taken up.

Table 9 shows the financial planning by the central governments of West Germany and the United States with their assumptions about real economic growth and unemployment, and compares these with the actual outturn.

In West Germany the margin of error of the assumed economic outturn widened sharply after 1976. Each time higher future growth rates were assumed than those currently achieved. Averaged out over seven financial plans, there was an overestimate of 100 per cent. The assumptions are officially called 'target projections', but in actual fact they were treated as forecasts. The underestimates of unemployment followed from the mistaken assumptions as to growth. The planners simply refused to believe that tax

Table 9 Central government medium-term financial planning in West Germany and the United States: target and actual economic outturn

Planning period	Real economic growth (% gross domestic product)		Percentage of unemployed	
	Target	Actual	Target	Actual
Federal Republic of Germany				
1976–80	4.5	3.5	3.0	4.2
1978–82	4.0	1.6	4.0	5.0
1980–4	3.0	0.9	–	7.0
1982–6	2–3	1.7	–	8.8
USA				
1979–83	3.8	1.3	5.3	8.0
1985–9	4.0	3.0[a]	–	–

[a] 1985–7.
Sources: DIW Weekly Report, 50, 1983; *Economic Impact*, 2, 1979; own calculations from OECD data.

revenues would not increase by the usual amount and that problems would not go away as much as they would have liked.

In the United States medium-term planning in 1979 was also based on the assumption that economic growth would again accelerate to an average 3.8 per cent, but economic growth proved to be only 1.3 per cent and unemployment, forecast at only 4 per cent for 1983, rose to 9.6 per cent.[30]

Even the planning-conscious Swedish government made the mistaken assumption that economic growth would accelerate during the 1970s (from 3.8 per cent in the first half of the decade to 4.3 per cent in the second half). In fact the growth rate turned sharply downwards, averaging out at only 2 per cent for the 1970s. It has to be said that this – long-term – forecast was made in 1971.[31] The new long-term forecast for the 1980s was distinctly more cautious and used two possible variants of the way the economy would develop, namely 1.6 and 1.9 per cent growth of gross domestic product in real terms.[32] This forecast proved to be realistic.

Is it just by chance that the West German and United States central governments displayed less ability to learn? In 1984 superpower America was banking on the economy performing in a way that outstripped serious forecasts by its optimism. The output of the economy was supposed to grow by an average of 4 per cent between 1985 and 1989, helping to reduce the state deficit.[33] Up to 1987 the economy had grown at 3 per cent, and still the financial planning for the period 1986–91 is working with growth rates of 3.5–4 per cent.[34]

Now it is in the nature of medium and long-term forecasts (especially the latter) to be fallible. This is not the problem that concerns us here. It would be easy for governments to make conservative forecasts, deliberately to use cautious assumptions and thus to have upper margins of error that in the 'worst' case would bring in a tax surplus. The fact that this so regularly does not occur says something about the decisional structures. The problem is twofold.

For one thing there is obviously a rooted disinclination to make realistic forecasts if these not only run counter to the forced optimism of large technocratic organizations but also inhibit the bureaucratic propensity to spend, as well as being less useful to the politicians. At all events, forecasting institutes that are dependent on government orders complain that they are pressured to be optimistic. Thus a spokesman for the IFO Institut said in 1984 at a conference of forecasting research experts: '. . . we are in no doubt about our function, which is to be "political wish-fulfilment assistants" '. He was referring to instructions received from the state in connection with forecasts, which 'for their part contain political objectives' and hence have a deceptive effect.[35] This was not contradicted by other commissioned forecasting researchers.

But the other and larger problem concerns the consequences of this mistaken forecasting. Whereas errors lead cautious financial planners to generate surpluses, the mistaken forecasts of optimistic planners result in deficits. With lower economic growth, tax receipts are lower than anticipated; and as unemployment is higher it occasions more expenditure, ranging from unemployment pay to social assistance or the costs of increased criminality. The answer given to these unplanned mismatches between expenditure and receipts is to issue loans.

To repeat: the simple solution to the problem would be conservative financial planning, which only risks producing unplanned surpluses. The magnitude of the difficulties encountered at this point is a sign of functional failure by the state. This means that the magnitude of the difficulties is due to structural causes. One of these is the unteachability of bureaucratic structures, which are used to solving every problem by economic growth instead of by reforms.

Conclusions and observation on the social costs of the world market

There is then an essential similarity between the crisis of state indebtedness and the pattern of state failure described here. It begins with political failure by the state in the shape of a failure to intervene. What usually happens is that neither the privileged recipient of income nor the unproductive capital is adequately taxed, nor are expenditures flowing into influential but unproductive sectors of society sufficiently curtailed. Indeed, problem-prone industries have been undertaxed for years, or have received excessive subsidies. Nor did the state shun the role of repair shop in general. Even the economy measures usually seemed to be aimed at combating symptoms. Jobs were shed in the lower income groups and savings were made on fringe groups such as pensioners, schoolchildren or the unemployed, or even the sick who, in addition to their compulsory insurance, were asked to contribute to health service costs. Economy measures have a habit of bypassing the income privileges of civil servants or the medical–industrial complex, thus becoming an unmistakable sign of a policy of hands off the no-go areas in society. In other words, the policy of economy was also an indirect surrender to positions of strength.

The wastefulness of the debt crisis and the economic failure it betokens are plain to see. Debt servicing is a major ingredient of the 'expensiveness' of the state and a constraint on its room for manoeuvre. High public debt drives up interest rates. Particularly in the early 1980s it encouraged the propensity of business enterprises to make financial investments, which do not create jobs. However, there is one branch of the economy that flourishes even on this state profligacy – the banking sector.

There is also functional state failure, especially in financial planning. If we disregard pensions, the problem of public indebtedness is not, as it might at first appear, a consequence of the 'expensive welfare state'. It is a consequence of the extent to which Western governments pay subsidies to entire sectors of the economy by their direct and indirect expenditures and receipts, whether it be the construction industry, agrobusiness, the energy sector, road transport or the banks. The picture clears sufficiently only when attention is turned from expenditures to receipts. The heavy taxation of the labour factor combined with relief for corporations, property and higher incomes also points to positions of strength and their concomitant no-go areas.

The trouble with studies of state finances is that they concentrate rigorously on expenditures by the state and ignore the taxes that are not paid. But 'tax expenditures' are an essential part of the subject. The *de facto* tacit tax privileges, consisting simply in the fact that taxes are not raised to appropriate levels – e.g. because they are based on absolute measures or units, such as cylinder capacity and litres, and not on (increasing) values – are still largely concealed. It may well be that these twilight zones are a field of activity much more congenial to the business lobby than state expenditures, which go through three readings in parliament and then are subject to scrutiny by the Public Accounts Committee.

However, tax reliefs for business, and grants to them, are not solely due to lobbying by business interests. Not for nothing have I placed so much emphasis on the significance of the functional positions, together with the power positions, in industrial society. Favourable treatment for businesses is usually based on an omnibus argument – that of the world market. The argument runs that business, and especially some industries or individual firms, must be relieved of cost burdens, either in order to counter competitive disadvantages or to compensate for price trends on the world market.

This is not the place to go into all the cases in which such arguments are simply pretexts. My contention is that the significance of the world market for state finances is greater and more critical than is commonly supposed. The myth of the world market is a primary component of the industrial system, especially from the viewpoint of the multinational superindustries. And yet very little is known about the costs to the economy and to public finances which a country has to pay for the extent and nature of its integration in the structure of the world economy. Nevertheless there are some indications that the social costs of such involvement are not small.

- In 1978 the political scientist Cameron published a remarkable study in which he revealed that, as external trade increases, so does the proportion of GNP taken up by state expenditures.[36]

- To this we may add that public indebtedness also shows a trend increase in countries more heavily involved in foreign trading compared with those which concentrate more on their domestic markets. Extreme examples are Belgium and Ireland: both countries are wide open to international trade, and both are heavily in debt.[37]
- The connection between involvement in world markets and growth in state expenditure can also be observed (since the 1960s) in East European countries.

It is reasonable to infer such a linkage if one considers governmental prepayments and consequential payments for the international economy. Payments have to be – or, at least, are – made in connection with research, education and infrastructure in the broadest sense by way of direct export subsidies and, not least, by tax exemptions. Consequential costs have to be paid when uncompetitive industries fail or when imported products cause difficulties.

Since most industrialized countries also compete in the world market for foreign investment, the prepayments include a suitable 'climate of investment' which more often than not has a cost aspect in addition to the waiver of financial demands. Tax concessions are widespread in this area. Consequential costs are paid if the capital is subsequently withdrawn or if the price of its continued presence is raised. Clearly, the sovereignty of the state *vis-à-vis* 'its' economy increases *pari passu* with the proportion of the productive capital owned by its nationals. This is the case in Japan, for example.

However, the argument of the world market with regard to state finances is not simply an argument of comparative analysis. It could well be that the increasing involvement of industrialized countries in world markets is encroaching upon the decisional freedom of all of them. Similarly, the social costs of integration in world markets could be on a rising trend for all of them. The costs of competitive subsidies for 'increasing competitiveness' alone are considerable,[38] and these costs bear no relationship to the potential benefit to the economy concerned. Often the only end result is that the same product is produced at a universally higher level of subsidy. This may promote overproduction, but it does nothing to lessen the number of losers from competitive subsidization.

If one country waives 50 per cent of taxes for its exporters this may give them a competitive advantage, but if everybody does the same this only results in making them all poorer by the amount of the lost tax revenue. If one country then goes further and grants its exporters complete tax exemption, all the other countries are disadvantaged on the export market despite having sacrificed vast amounts of tax revenue.

The same arguments apply to policies aimed at attracting industry as to interventions forgone for the sake of a 'good climate of investment'. What is involved is the somewhat cutthroat competition among national states in a largely unregulable world market. Business enterprises have a tendency to form cartels when competition would be harmful to all of them, whereas international politics have not so far been able to engender such cooperative action among states. Thus national states continue to compete on the world market and pay their common tribute to a third party – superindustry with its worldwide nexus of interests. To this third party we shall now turn our attention.

8 Superindustrialism and Post-industrialism

Two scenarios

State failure is the result of two processes working in opposite directions. It arises because an increased need of regulation on the part of industrial societies coincides with a declining trend in the ability of the state and politics to regulate. The increased need for regulation is the consequence of the structural crisis of an industrialism which has reached the limits of its development, and the problems of regulation are the result of a position of power built up by this same industrialism. The two phenomena need to be considered separately: the former is related to the crisis of a method of production, and the latter concerns the rigidities of a power constellation. In one case it is related to 'superindustrialism' and in the other it concerns the 'tank syndrome'.

By 'superindustrialism' I mean the phase of industrialism which began with the post-war boom and which ran into crisis in the 1970s. It is the stage which, according to forecasts made in the 1960s, should be followed by the 'post-industrial society'. The real question is whether this consummation will occur or whether there will be open conflict between the superindustrial and post-industrial trends. In most Western countries the two trends are both juxtaposed and opposed. Which of them will prevail is the fundamental question of the future for these societies.

What is so appealing about the theory of the 'post-industrial society' is that there was at least the concept of such a society before the debate in the 1970s about the environment and raw materials.[1] Later, Daniel Bell identified it as having five characteristics, namely,

1 Economic sector: the change from a goods-producing to a service economy.
2 Occupational distribution: the pre-eminence of the professional and technical class.

3 Axial principle: the centrality of technical knowledge as the source of innovation and of policy formation for the society.
4 Future orientation: the control of technology and technological assessment.
5 Decision-making: the creation of a new 'intellectual technology'.[2]

There can be no doubt that this was an early recognition not only of
objective possibilities but also of actual trends in the developed industrial
societies, even though it was inter-mixed with a good proportion of euphoria
and overestimation of the role of intellectuals in ensuring the triumph of
reason. The trend towards services and knowledge-intensive production was
correctly foreseen, but the preparedness of many countries to face the future
was overestimated. Moreover, the problems of industrialism still persisting
were underestimated.

It was the persistence of these problems that led Herman Kahn, who had
been an adherent of the concept of post-industrialism, to adopt an opposite
position as a result of the Harrisburg disaster in 1979, that of the 'super-
industrial society'. Kahn attributes two main characteristics to this society.
First, because of the large dimensions of its enterprises and the risks of its
technology it is 'problem prone' and, second, it is marked by the extent of the
'externalities' it creates, especially external costs. Kahn talks about the 'rise of
a worldwide industrial economy, in which projects have become so gigantic
that the external or unintended effects . . . may become greater than the
primary (or intended) products. Unless the influence of the super-industrial
economy on the social and physical environment is brought under control, it
will permeate, and perhaps destroy, everything.'[3]

I employ the two concepts 'superindustrialism' and 'post-industrialism' not
because of an uncritical attitude towards Daniel Bell or Herman Kahn, but
because I believe that Bell's idea of a series of stages from industrialism to
post-industrialism is just as important as the shocked discovery of the professional optimist Kahn that the problems of industrialism have not gone away.
In the light of the Chernobyl catastrophe, and the controversy which that
catastrophe touched off in the East and the West, I stay with these two
concepts.

Two scenarios can be deduced from each of these concepts.[4] First, the
scenario of post-industrialism. This posits a series of stages in which the
dominance of the industrial production of goods that has existed hitherto is
terminated by the services and information economy in the same way as
industry replaced agriculture in the past. However, such a scenario would be
of significance for ecology and structural policy only if the 'hard' risk-bearing
forms of industry were reduced, and not only at the level of employment but
also in actual production.

The scenario of post-industrialism is a scenario of qualitative growth. This is growth accompanied by equal or lower consumption of non-renewable resources and an equal or reducing level of external problem effects, from health protection to state finances. The post-industrial scenario describes one of two realistically possible lines of development for developed societies.

This means that we are not thinking about a kind of 'ideal' process of social development. Post-industrialism is in the first place only ecologically beneficial, in that it saves raw materials, relieves stress on the environment and offers new opportunities for employment. This is by no means negligible, but in itself it says nothing about the *quality* of the services and information which will now become dominant. So far the promises of an 'information society' seem to point rather in the direction of a 'disinformation society',[5] and some of the proliferating services are anything but hopeful signs.

Therefore the post-industrialism scenario is not intended to do more than describe real possibilities of development within the framework of existing conditions but, unless preparations are made to switch to this line of development, more humane forms of services and more enlightened forms of information will not be possible. (In other words, a second change of direction will then be required.)

The second scenario, that of superindustrialism, characterizes a future in which traditional ways of producing goods continue and develop alongside the services and information sector. In this model of development the 'tertiary sector' plays in the main a preparatory and nuisance-abatement role for the goods-producing industry that remains dominant and continues to determine the pace of development, which in the long term will prove to be unstable (table 10), for the structural problems which surfaced during the 1970s are not really being overcome. The strategy of growth at the expense of the state finances is not being abandoned, and sufficient jobs are not being created. The level of externalized risks and costs remains high, and as the price of raw materials on the world market falls so resource consumption, which had fallen on account of rising raw materials prices, is once more on the increase.

What is really interesting about the 'post-industrial society' is not the numerous lines of development that point in its direction but the extent to which the structures of superindustry are proving to be stable, blocking the thrust towards innovation in that direction. This calls for a more detailed explanation.

Superindustrialism

Herman Kahn believes that the phenomenon of superindustrialism became apparent only in the 1970s, but there is good reason to apply the term to the

Table 10 Superindustrialism and post-industrialism compared

Superindustrialism	Post-industrialism
Highest phase of traditional industrialism transforming non-renewable raw materials into harmful substances and waste	Preponderance of non-material production of information and services
1 *Quantitative growth*: 'High volume'; long-term limits to growth	1 *Qualitative growth*: 'High value'; 'Growth of the limits'; Resource economy
2 Strong *centralization* of capital and power through post-war cycle industries; trend towards large-scale capital-intensive projects	2 Great importance of new small and medium sized enterprises; knowledge-intensive production, *more decentralization*
3 *Rigidity* ('tank syndrome')	3 *Innovation*: Flexibility ('bicycle syndrome')
4 Preponderance of the *world market* and *superpowers*	4 Enhanced importance of *regional structures*
5 Strong *external problem effects*; environmental and accident risks; large quantities of waste	5 More *appropriate production* structures: more environmentally friendly technologies and types of economy; smaller quantities of wastes
6 Growing *damage-repair* sectors of industry and state 'living' on problems of industrialism; symptom-combating propensity	6 More forethought and preventive action

industrial structures which have developed in the post-war phase, the 'long wave' which has since reached its trough.

One of the distinguishing marks of the industrial structure of super-industrialism is the presence of leading multinational corporations, especially the oil and energy groups. There are also the automobile groups, the chemicals and electricity groups and the large steel corporations. These powerful branches of industry also form among themselves an interdependent nexus of interests. There is also the armaments industry, which has achieved a strong position within both military blocs and has had increasing success with exports to Third World countries. It is based preponderantly on the industrial structure described above. Whilst the construction industry does not have a dominant position in the world market, it has traditionally enjoyed a strong position within its own domestic markets in the industrial countries, with a strong bent towards cartel formation. In any event it too is one of the successful industries of the post-war cycle.

The phase of the world economy marked by this cycle is sometimes referred to as 'late industrialism'. This concept carries the significant implication that in this phase industrialism is in any case reaching the limits of its potentialities, especially the potentiality for expansion of the production of goods on the basis of finite resources and increasing spoliation of the environment. However, concepts such as this, which imply forecasts, raise problems. The same applies to the concept of 'late capitalism', which otherwise addresses important structural and legitimation crises of industrial capitalism at this stage.[6] Another description of the phase of the development of capitalism in the post-war era is that of 'state interventionism'. This emphasizes the importance now possessed by the state's policy of growth, together with various welfare functions of the state. All I object to in this is the idea of intervention, because in this phase the state is 'intervening' less and less, if 'intervening' means taking decisions running counter to the trend.

A third designation for this post-war phase of Western industrialism is that of 'state monopoly capitalism'. Like the previous designation it is of marxist origin, and it also stresses the growing importance of the state as a crisis manager and a source of growth, since all the other sources, especially that of expansion on the world market, have already been fully exploited. This phase presupposes the 'monopoly capitalism' of the previous long economic cycle. According to this theory the centralized and worldwide established industries make use of national states, at the expense of small enterprises and the 'broad mass of the workers'.[7] The American marxist O'Connor adds that this is the phase of increased 'tax exploitation', of the expansion of 'social industries' and finally of the 'financial crisis of the state'.[8]

These are important aspects of the way things are going, and important characteristics of the current phase. Especially relevant is the observation of an increasing load placed upon the state by centralized capital. The concept of superindustrialism, which I prefer, is intended over and above this to highlight the problems posed by the mode of production.

In any event this stage of industrialism is marked by an extreme intensification of the lines of industrial development:

- increased production of goods using finite resources
- centralization of capital and decisions
- specialization

- risk proneness
- externalization of problems and costs
- unregulability
- instrumentalization of the state.

Superindustrialism is the elevation of these trends of development to the final point of a fundamental structural crisis, and it strikes at the industrial heart of capitalism (under its state capitalism guise as well). In terms of crisis theory it has been increasingly obvious since the beginning of the 1970s through a build-up of malfunctions including raw materials shortages, environmental crises, mass unemployment, financial crises, structural crises and crises of acceptability and legitimation.

Superindustry is a production method of industrial capitalism with several novel attributes. The huge size of industrial groups is novel, and so is the volume of the world market. Although the world market has existed for a long time, previously it was dominated by individual nations, whereas now it is dominating the policy of national states – of all national states. Planning and projects now have a new order of magnitude – and so have the major industrial risks. They are different in kind, and not only in the armaments sector. Through nuclear and chemical waste products or their effects on climate they influence generations in the distant future.

Never before in history has production been carried on so indiscriminately at the expense of future generations, and the exploitation has taken new forms. Nowadays its ruinous aspects, such as exploitation to destruction, are sometimes held in check by workforces organized in trade unions, although this applies less to the exploitation of nature. A new field for exploitation is provided by state finances and future generations. The rates of economic growth achieved by superindustrialism in its expansionary phase are historically unique too – but the limits to growth which it has finally encountered are also historically unique, and the resultant crisis has been correspondingly all-embracing.

Superindustrialism is characterized by several limits to growth, which post-industrialism will reach only much later, if ever.

First there is the resource basis. Traditional industry grew large on non-renewable raw materials such as coal, oil and ores. Contrary to earlier assumptions of the 'Club of Rome', these resources will not be exhausted in the near future; however, the more they are used up, the more expensive they are to obtain. The increasing use of water is another activity subject to this law of steeply rising resource costs. Even in agriculture the intensive use of resources leads to disproportionate cost increases. The limits of quantitative growth are also becoming apparent with respect to the resource of building land, the price of which is rising steeply in densely populated areas because of its perceived scarcity.

In contrast, post-industrialism experiences smaller raw materials problems by the very fact that it produces mainly information and services, which are non-material things. However, even individual products contain relatively less raw material and more information. They are becoming relatively smaller in volume but higher in value.

Superindustry is pressing against not only cost barriers, but also barriers of governability. Its unregulability has led to a considerable rise in the problem level of industrial society, and it routinely externalizes problems and their costs. At the same time the high problem level has created pressing needs which are bound to interest specialized nuisance abatement technocracies on account of the public demand for them.

It was apparent by the end of the 1970s, however, that industrial societies, which to a large extent create problems *and* make a living out of them, would not come through this questionable cycle unscathed. The consequences of uncontrolled chemicalization, motorization, electrification or in-company rationalization might for a time provide employment for specialist damage-repair industries and bureaucracies, but there were financial limits to this marketing and nationalization of the problems of industrial society – limits which also applied to the socialization of demand in areas where (as in building) demand was approaching saturation limits. They also apply to many other areas, including the costs of a growing central bureaucracy with its income privileges.

Thus with regard to the finances of states too, what was originally a condition for the success of the industrial boom during the post-war cycle finally turned into an obstacle to further development. The same applies to the power structure of superindustrialism, which was built up and finally consolidated in this period. This has such negative effects, especially on the innovative potential of industry, that it requires separate treatment (see p. 107ff).

Superindustrialism is also characterized by certain myths which are not conducive to a structural change in the direction of a different post-industrial model of development.

There is first the myth of industry, which alleges that industrial production of goods alone creates prosperity and that the services sector only makes its living by redistributing this prosperity. This myth is persisting most obstinately at present in the state socialism countries of Eastern Europe. Yet it was also extremely persistent even in countries which after 1973 showed ten years of zero growth industrially (such as West Germany). Its effects even reach into the statistics, which in many countries are statistics of industry although the greater part of gross domestic product has for long been produced in the services sector.

The myth of industry ignores facts such as the following. During the 1970s, whilst industrial production was frequently stagnating, the services sector became the engine of growth in many Western countries. During this period private services, e.g. in Sweden, achieved a remarkable increase in productivity. The myth of industry also has a one-sided fixation on the export of goods – whereas there has long since developed a rapidly expanding world market for services (and information) estimated to have been worth $600,000 million in 1985. Furthermore, an increasing number of 'peripheral countries' are now joining the ranks of the exporters of services.[9] In the United States 22.4 million jobs were created in the service industries between 1970 and 1984, whilst the numbers employed in industry remained unchanged. But most importantly, this tertiary sector is now an essential factor in increasing the productivity of the economy as a whole. This applies to agriculture, to industry and preeminently to the services sector itself. It is particularly training intensive, and even its production equipment is strongly knowledge intensive. In many economies, services for the services sector are growing in importance.

The second characteristic of superindustrialism is the myth of high rates of growth. This does not refer simply to the historically high rates of growth during the post-war cycle. It relates to the consequences of what is called later in this book the 'tank syndrome'. The more unregulatable and unable to reform themselves economies and states become, the more they tend to seek solutions to problems such as mass unemployment or indebtedness not with structural measures but by pinning their hopes on high economic growth. We have already met this phenomenon in state financial planning in West Germany and the United States. Moreover, as the capacity for reform decreases, so the inclination to pay an excessive price (e.g. in state indebtedness) for higher growth rates increases. In this connection it should be recalled that the developed industrial societies earn a considerable absolute increment in affluence even when growth rates are low.

There is thirdly the myth of laissez-faire. This is the philosophy of an industrial power structure which wants to be left in peace. It is a permanent part of what is termed later on the 'tank syndrome'. Ultimately it amounts to the concept of private responsibility for investment and public liability for the problems resulting therefrom. It is a myth because an economy of this type makes its living increasingly both from the state and its budgets, and thus makes increasing demands on state assistance. It is the *economy* that has involved the state heavily in the production process. For this reason it is difficult to see why the state should not be entitled to intervene by taking long-term measures to avert crises – including its own crises of finance and legitimation.

Only passing reference will be made here to other myths of superindustrialism. The monopolist industries brazenly protest their love of the 'market economy'. Then there is the myth of the world market, referred to earlier, the social costs of which to the state are higher than they appear to be. The myth of large scale has long since proved to be questionable.[10]

Lastly I quote an official Japanese report to illustrate that beyond such myths enlightened technocracies are well aware of the limits of industrialism and the outlook for post-industrialism:

> Until towards the end of the sixties the Japanese economy had a high growth rate. . . . This was due to the unusual growth rates of a rapid expansion of the whole world economy, adequate supplies of cheap raw materials and energy from abroad, technology taken over from abroad and the rise of mass consumer markets into which mainly durable consumer goods were sold. However, in the seventies increasing difficulties were experienced in obtaining raw materials and energy, and trade did not go so smoothly as it had previously. The environment and the conditions that had so favoured the high growth rates of the Japanese economy changed . . . less emphasis was placed on material satisfactions for all wants. The quest was rather for a better quality of life. The services industry became increasingly important, and the structures of industry altered their shape. Information has become more important compared with physical raw materials.[11]

It remains to add that in no other country did the excesses of industrialism become so tangible (with the exception of the East European countries). There was no alternative to a change of direction – this would have been dictated by shortage of materials alone. Notwithstanding a substantial structural change between 1973 and 1983 the myth of industrial growth is still very potent in Japan itself, although it has been redirected to knowledge-intensive goods. It is the Scandinavian countries that have the more interesting experience with regard to post-industrialism.

Post-industrialism

Post-industrialism begins as a side-effect of industrialism and continues as a product of crisis, but it ends by offering valid alternatives to industrialism.

At first the trend to post-industrialism largely follows the prevailing course of events. It consists of above-average growth of the 'tertiary sector', i.e. production, other than agriculture and industry. This 'services sector' begins by fulfilling very important functions for the large industries. This is true of banking and insurance as well as education and research or trade and transport. It is especially true of all kinds of repair functions.

So it is industry that first creates a growing requirement for services (always including information services). If things develop favourably, this demand of productive industry becomes transformed increasingly to a demand for innovative services, especially expertise, research and development affecting new, more appropriate especially resource-saving technologies. This innovative variant of services is dominant in post-industrialism. The share of the materials and energy-producing basic industries recedes and that of the knowledge-creating sectors of the economy grows. Renewable raw materials and energies also become increasingly important.

It is an essential hallmark of post-industrialism that the services sector becomes increasingly important to the productivity of the economy

1 for an ecologically more appropriate agriculture, aiming not at quantity but at quality in its products and production methods,
2 for a socially and ecologically more appropriate industry, achieving its successes through knowledge-intensive products,
3 for the services sector itself – productivity here is frequently low, offering new opportunities of achieving higher efficiency through more 'intelligent' organization and consultancy activities.

The post-industrial trend also includes an independent demand for services, however, brought about by the longer life expectancy of the population and by the increase in leisure time. A potent factor in the rise of this demand has been the strengthening of the post-material trend. This has many causes, ranging from the increase in service occupations or changes in the time budget of the population as a whole to the increasing importance of psychotherapy or self-realization.

The post-material trend represents above all a change of values aiming at quality of life, with a strong relativization of material goods consumption and the standards of industrial society such as performance, hierarchy etc. In many places the post-material trend is becoming concentrated into an alternative opposition to the problems resulting from super-industrialism.

This alternative movement has grown up inside the existing party system in countries such as Japan and the United States. In West Germany, Holland, Denmark or Italy it has produced independent parties operating outside the established party system. It exists even in countries such as Hungary, Poland and East Germany as a political opposition movement.

The alternative movement is the typical opposition movement in the crisis phase of superindustrialism. The movement is the political negation of super-industrialism's specific susceptibility to problems, its gigantomania, its 'tonnes ideology', its destruction of nature, its risks affecting future generations and its increases of crisis proportions in productivity and destructivity.

The alternative movement is at the same time the specific opposition to the failing state, which, instead of taking timely preventive action, repairs the damage afterwards, priding itself on its growth policies. The alternative opposition stems in essence from the realization that the political system of the developed industrial societies does not adequately fulfil vital protective functions and fails to give a sufficient lead on matters that are essential to survival. It is also a sign of the conspicuous incapacity of the developed industrial societies for reform and innovation.

The alternative movement is in many respects 'fundamental opposition'. Yet many of its aims can be ranked with those of the post-industrial movement and strengthen the movement. It has often awakened a response among the general public far beyond the ranks of its own membership.

The post-industrial tendency has become highly visible in many countries since the beginning of the 1970s, and even earlier in the United States. This is due mainly to the following developments.

(1) There has been a shift to post-material values of quality of life and self-realization.

(2) More important is the trend towards services (including information services). During the last 20 years 72 million jobs have been created in service industries in the Western industrial countries. Nearly 70 per cent of all Americans work in such industries and earn a corresponding proportion of the gross domestic product. Nearly all new jobs are created in those industries, whilst unemployment occurs predominantly in the old smoke-stack industries.[12]

(3) In most of the Western countries small and medium- sized enterprises have replaced the jobs that were systematically shed through rationalization in the large-scale industries. (Some of these were alternative enterprises with a definite ecological bias). The US Small Business Administration estimates that between 1980 and 1982 all net new jobs were created in firms with fewer than 100 employees. Other surveys have estimated the proportion as being from 53 to 70 per cent.[13] In most cases the largest growth was found in small businesses. Medium-sized and small businesses are also responsible for a considerable amount of innovation.

(4) Industry itself was under strong pressure to change to resource-saving processes, knowledge- and service-intensive methods of production and experiments with more decentralized and participative organizational structures.[14]

These trends have been visible to differing degrees. They are most visible in the Scandinavian countries, less so in the EEC countries and least of all in Eastern Europe. It is still believed in industrial technocratic circles that the leading role played by the services sector as an engine of growth is a sign of crisis, which has to be countered by moves towards neo-industrialization. It is at present an open question whether this movement towards reindustrialization in the guise of superindustry may yet succeed in becoming established.

The crucial question: the quality of the information and services of the future

This unresolved issue is the first reason for not yielding too readily to euphoria about post-industrialization,[15] a trend which, it must be clearly reiterated, is advantageous to the environment or structural policy only if it is more than simply an epiphenomenon of a continued or rekindled growth of the 'hard' industries of the post-war cycle. Jobless industrial growth with a services sector as a universal nuisance abater is not ecologically, economically or sociologically a meaningful prospect.

Even if it should become established, however, the scenario of post-industrialism is not as such an ideal course for society to take regardless of whatever ecological advantages it may have. All it does is offer objective possibilities of politically more progressive and humane conditions. The manner in which the services and information economies have developed so far gives rise to two problems in particular, which suggest a third scenario of a humane post-industrialism.

One of the problems is the possibility that more and more people will be less and less in demand, whilst ever-increasing demands are placed upon fewer and fewer people. Present trends seem increasingly likely to result in a highly specialized 'expertocracy' that becomes a privileged minority, in contrast with the broad mass of low-skilled or even 'superfluous' people. These trends, partly foreseen by Daniel Bell, are unmistakably present. The other trend of 'realistic' post-industrialism is that of commercialization in the information industry. A society guided in the main by information put out by vested capitalist interests could in the extreme case be at risk of falling for a total ideology, for the countervailing movement to the failure of the pure market is not only the activities of the state, insufficient as ever. Rather, in parliamentary systems the existence of a critical public forum, i.e. a relatively independent forum, has an essential part to play at least in the area of detecting faults and giving guidance for future action. If this function were to be dissolved in the shortsighted blinkered vision of market interests, such societies would lose the essential precondition of a long-term outlook. There would then be the prospect of a 'disinformation society', in which the short-term view of the market imposes a short-term view of policy, more than is the case already. In that case Daniel Bell's criterion of the post-industrial society – orientation to the future – would not be fulfilled.

No – the scenario of post-industrialism is really not much more than a description of certain trends and possibilities. Everything depends upon whether and how they are translated into policies.

9 Tank Syndrome and Bicycle Syndrome

Innovation and stagnation

It may be debatable whether the industrial countries can rely in the long term only on the development potential of the knowledge- and service-intensive resource-saving production methods of post-industrialism, but nobody denies that long-term recovery after the structural crisis of the 1970s and 1980s depends upon thoroughgoing innovation and, as with services, with innovations the question is no longer whether they are occurring, but whether they are so all-pervasive as to offer the prospect of overcoming the crisis. Industrialism may be able to take advantage of a few of the post-industrial developments and so get by fairly satisfactorily, until the next recession administers a rude awakening from its dream of a comeback. A certain mix of technical innovations (microelectronics, biotechnology, materials technology and computer-aided processes of all kinds) might be pushed ahead frantically by all the industrial countries and still not avail to counterbalance the decline of the old industries sufficiently to produce a lasting recovery for all the industrial countries.

In other words, structural change and the process of innovation must already demonstrate a considerable efficacy in order to produce an effect in overcoming the crisis. As we have already emphasized, crises create pressure for change. They can lead to new productive solution by way of innovation.

Historically, crisis has always been the decisive engine of development, but the experience of history has always shown that the crisis mechanism lost its productive potency in entrenched power and privilege structures and failed to issue in further development.

During the last few years long-range forecasts for the capitalist industrial countries have increasingly given cause to work with two typical scenarios: that of long-term recovery after the structural crisis of the 1970s and 1980s, and that of long-term stagnation.[1]

A number of plausible arguments could be advanced in favour of the optimistic scenario of a long-term upswing:

- the 'long-wave' theory, that of the 50–60 year cycles which the Russian economist Kondratieff traced back to the French revolution – according to this theory we should have a long period of climb before us, after the trough lasting from 1973 to 1983;[2]
- the innovation theory, linked to that of Kondratieff, which expects to find an 'innovative thrust' in the troughs of long waves, and can point to such innovations at the present;[3]
- a climate of change, which is gathering pace even in the shape of 'conservative reform' and is producing new ideas ranging from environmental protection to the question of decentralization;[4]
- changes in the conditions surrounding production, which have at least revived the propensity to invest.

All this gives the scenario of long-term recovery and innovation real credibility. Only a foolish forecaster would ignore this possibility in favour of global pessimism.

Nevertheless it is just as essential to consider the following questions.

- What must the innovation process achieve in economic and ecological terms with respect to the existing structural crisis?
- What would be the characteristics of a process of innovation capable of initiating a new phase of development in the industrial societies of the West?
- What are the structural barriers to comprehensive innovation in these societies, and to what extent can they be overcome?

Levels of technology and barriers to innovation

Technology is not only a question of 'hardware', and innovations of long-term economic cycles have to do with more than this type of technology. By technology I mean the planned construction of purpose-designed tools on the basis of invented patterns. Material technology shapes materials. Social technology, or social engineering, shapes social behaviour (also in the form of self-organization). There is also intellectual technology, which 'organizes' information and makes knowledge out of it. Gottl-Ottlilienfeld[5] has made a distinction of this sort. He refers to *'Realtechnik'*, *'Sozialtechnik'* and

'Intellektualtechnik'. And as long ago as 1935 Karl Mannheim, significantly perhaps in the trough of the last 'long wave', pointed out the importance of social engineering and innovations in social techniques such as democratic planning.[6]

We are more familiar with technology in the form of hardware than with social discoveries and the corresponding dimensions of social engineering, but in fact what is known as technical progress has always been accompanied by discoveries in social engineering. This is true not only of increasing productivity in factories. Increasing military destructiveness too has always a social engineering dimension. Napoleon not only possessed better firearms than the armies of the continental absolute monarchies; he also encountered their parade-ground formations (which perfectly reflected the late-absolutist tank syndrome) with open flexible attack formations. This simple social innovation contributed to his success, as did also the use of new techniques of propaganda. Then in Spain he himself was confronted by the social innovation of guerilla tactics. These examples show that social engineering like the other types of technology, offers a variety of possibilities of development. Social engineering includes production by division of labour, and the invention of the team group or the self-managed alternative enterprise. It includes discoveries aimed at increasing centralization and bureaucratization as well as the institution of parliament and the techniques of 'occupations' and 'sit ins', the hunger strike and the citizen's initiative. Social engineering includes both the centralized transport network and the invention of pedestrianized areas.

Intellectual technology includes not only questionnaires, 'paradigms' and scientific methods. It ranges from 'brainstorming' to the computer program, from the system concept to self-awareness training. And it should also include prior information about the socioeconomically conditioned nature of knowledge. Its importance for society is increased by the simultaneous presence of an excess and a deficiency of knowledge in times of rapid social change.

The correlation between innovations in technical science and social science was rediscovered in the 1970s, significantly enough during the trough of a 'long wave'. The economic and technological stagnation, described by Gerhard Mensch in 1975 as a 'technological stalemate',[7] was bound in time to throw up questions about the social structures in which these phenomena were found – although such questions were surprisingly infrequent.

Thus technological stalemate was complemented by 'institutional sclerosis', a concept which the OECD took over in 1979 from Mancur Olson in a futurology study.[8] From this concept came the conservative formulation of 'Eurosclerosis'. It was mainly employed to combat the role of the trade unions and the welfare state in Europe, but its proposed strategy of lower wages, smaller social benefits and hence more poverty was scarcely able to solve the problem of innovation. What we need to know is which of the

social structures are obstructing the innovation process in material technology, for the answer to that will tell us where social innovations need to be
made.

It is a mystery how Kondratieff's long-term cycles could be studied without
any consideration of the changes in the structures of society connected with
them. Did not the first of these cycles begin at the time of the American and
French revolutions? And did not the next cycle begin with the 1848 revolution? Did not extensive reforms, such as Bismarck's social legislation, play a
part in the trough of the next long wave? Did not the recovery after the trough
of the 1930s begin with the innovation of the welfare state, with Keynesian
demand management and similar institutional innovations? And was not the
trough of the 1970s fundamentally due to a failure of the traditional institutional structure of the state and the economy?

The thesis of Olson in the OECD study just mentioned, and of other
authors such as Alexander King[9] is basically that of the neo-liberal variant of
the critique of simultaneous failure of the market and the state. Brought to its
discussible point, the idea is somewhat as follows. The market suffers from
monopolies and arrangements which hamper innovation and reduce flexibility. It fails to meet the challenge of the future and to satisfy the public interest
and the necessities of the external economy (OECD). And, like the market, the
state has an excessively short-term outlook, is dependent upon powerful
interest groups and encounters all sorts of intractable resistances. The public
goods it produces are too expensive. Social innovations ought to overcome
these 'social rigidities' (Olson). The areas of these social innovations range
from the state and its educational systems via corporate structures and the attitudes of employers and labour to the institutions of the capital market or
foreign trade. Only when the ambient conditions within society are radically
changed will fundamentally new technical paradigms be able to prevail.

But what does this mean? Clearly, 'social innovators' who have nothing else
in mind than to reduce social security contributions and wages – together
with taxes on corporations – on the pretext of reestablishing the market to
give free rein to the old economy are simply a part of the problem that has to be
solved.

A process of innovation that will really overcome the crisis has not only to
embrace all three levels of technology. It must also influence the relevant
conditions of the social structure. I believe that in this connection the inter-
action of innovations in material and social technology with the processes of
power formation are of critical importance.

On this subject I advance four propositions.[10]

Proposition one: technology of any kind can only be understood in conjunc-
tion with the social structure of those who use it. The set of their interests

determines the different purposes for which the tools are used and their power structures determine the kind of technology. Hierarchical centralized systems tend to evolve a different 'technological culture' from decentralized or participative systems.

Proposition two: technology, whether material – scientific, social or intellectual, develops cyclically. An innovative phase is followed by an establishment phase which leads on to the phase of obsolescence. The long-term trend of this process of development is towards an increasingly autonomous and inappropriate technology. As it becomes widely applied, so the patterns that were once innovative become 'institutionalized' and in the long run more and more ossified. In the sphere of material technology this is true of the manufacture of goods and production equipment. In the sphere of social engineering this is true of social or political institutions. In the sphere of intellectual technology this is true of scientific methods, paradigms etc.[11]

Proposition three: it is not, however, the technologies or the institutions that make themselves autonomous, obsolete or inappropriate, but the people who use them. Behind this autonomizing or stagnation effect there are concealed processes of establishment and power accumulation. Even the superficially attractive proposition that technical innovations presuppose institutional innovations overlooks the fact that institutional reforms too are repeatedly defeated by the rigidities of hierarchical power in the economy or the state.

Proposition four: because of this, innovation or stagnation is primarily a subject for 'kratology' – the study of power. Power accumulation processes generally begin with fundamental technical and institutional innovations. New enterprises start up with new products and processes. New political movements rise with proposals for structural change. However, at some point in the trend it becomes evident that power is itself a brake on innovation.

The dilemma posed for innovation by power is the result of a fourfold privilege. First, power is the privilege of not having to be intelligent. Problems can be solved by calling in additional resources, so that they do not necessitate additional intellectual effort. Second, power is the privilege of a diminished pressure of reality. According to Karl Deutsch, in a certain sense, power is 'the ability to afford not to learn.'[12] Third, power is the privilege of a lessened pressure for acceptance; Max Weber says that it is characterized by the ability to get one's way even against resistance. Fourth, power is the privilege of an increased chance of redistribution, which means that, with power, material success is not governed only by achievement and good ideas.

I have given the designation of 'tank syndrome' to the innovation dilemma of power. A tank driver can be stupid and blind. Unlike a cyclist he does not have to make an intelligent response to the obstacles posed by the environment. Problems are 'externalized'. It is the environment, not the tank driver, that bears the brunt. With the cyclist, in contrast, the problems of riding badly are fully internalized. In his case the rule is 'he who causes, pays', unlike the tank syndrome, in which society has to pay for the damage.

The *bicycle syndrome* is characterized by an intelligent attitude which handles the situation from a position of weakness. This, incidentally, is akin to the explanation of the successful evolution of the human race as an intelligent species.

For a long time the tank driver has the advantage, but the problems he encounters in the end, whether insurmountable obstacles or lack of fuel, are more serious than those of cyclist.

I am straining the analogy in order to describe the inertial momentum of hierarchical centralism as it has developed to a more or less marked degree in the various industrial societies. The point to grasp is the inertia and non-innovative ways of reacting that are made possible, though not inevitable, by power situations. There is no law which says that the people at the top of large hierarchies should not be open to change, full of ideas and cooperative, but the way to such a consummation is hard and the hopes for enlightened monarchs, liberal general secretaries and 'modern' top managers are frequently a reflection of the social structure nourishing such hopes rather than of its potential for reform. Why should the political culture of a country not operate more favourably? However, the political culture itself is moulded by the social structures – often with a considerable cultural lag.

Nevertheless there are doubtless some factors that may modify the rigidity and egocentricity of hierarchical organizations – the tradition of a country, a marked propensity for consensus, well-tried processes of cooperation, countervailing powers and internal checks on the power of large organizations. In organizations with well-established rights of codetermination the pressure of the outside world can as a rule be better transmitted. An economy with mixed corporations (conglomerates), which are more adaptable because (unlike simple car, construction or electricity generating enterprises) they have a wider range of possibilities, also enjoys a more beneficial effect. These are all important modifications which explain the differing patterns of behaviour in the organizational fabric of an industrial society. The most important modifier of behaviour is crisis.

The tank syndrome explains why the crisis mechanism takes effect so late and so often unsatisfactorily. It explains the widespread tendency to production under the protection of subsidies – or even of the police. It explains the propensity to react to problems of acceptance by increasing indoctrination and propaganda. It explains the defects (and the competitive disadvantages) of the East European economies. It explains the stupidities of the American automobile industry when faced with the oil crisis. It explains the foolish behaviour of the European automobile industry at a time of crisis in the environment. It explains the ignorance of the electricity industry with respect to intelligent energy techniques. Last but not least, it explains the inflexible 'carry on' strategies, particularly those of the nuclear industry in Western and Eastern Europe after Harrisburg and Chernobyl.

The contrast between the tank syndrome and the bicycle syndrome becomes clear if we compare the way in which the Scandinavian countries came through the structural crisis of the 1960s with what happened in the United Kingdom.

In the case of the United Kingdom nearly all the important social protagonists – the Prime Minister foremost among them – acted the tank syndrome part, being rigid, egocentric and ready to fight to the bitter end. Power structures that were as full of tradition as they were ossified lay at the root of this behaviour. All the protagonists tended to reserve their original positions with little disposition to learn, and to concentrate on maintaining or improving their position in the power and perks hierarchy. Agitation and propaganda were features of public life, with a strong preponderance on the conservative side. Thus there was little motivation and acceptance. This structure was responsible for a dramatic decline.[13] The level of social conflict was correspondingly high and the inclination to transfer social friction to the international level was just as strong. Hence the very high expenditure on armaments.

The Scandinavian model should not be idealized as a contrast with the foregoing, but the fact that the five Nordic countries have come through the difficult structural crisis since 1973 with a relatively successful environmental policy and the highest level of employment among Western countries is due to structural causes; a comparatively active modernizing role of the state, strong municipalities, traditions of participation and cooperation, no tradition of colonial exploitation, a relatively well-developed information sector and generally speaking more manageable orders of size. Internationally too they tend to take a cooperative stance.

Japan too came through the structural crisis of the 1970s more or less successfully with the state playing an active role, a relatively consensus-oriented political culture (with the Narita airport conflict constituting an exception and a salutary shock), cooperative business management, comparatively active municipalities and low expenditure on armaments.

Crises that do not lead to development?

The tank syndrome denotes a constellation of crucial importance to further development in the industrial countries, which could also be described as a distorted crisis mechanism. The rigid power structures of hierarchized centralism characteristically become alerted to crises too late. Their capacity for shelving problems is what causes them to fail for long periods to react appropriately to pressure for change.

So the question is not simply whether hierarchized centralism is propitious soil for innovation at all, but also whether innovations are introduced in time. The longer a process of adaptation is put off, the more expensive it becomes: it begins with subsidies for products that would no longer sell without the subsidy, and it continues with the social costs that arise because others have reacted more quickly and are now taking advantage of the technical backwardness of the subsidized product.

Now it would be possible for the state to raise the diminished pressure for change impinging on large industrial organizations by taking preemptive action. It is a fact that an active policy on the environment, energy and structures has had effects of this kind in Japan or Sweden. Contrary to the *laissez-faire* myth, innovations have been stimulated in this way. Moreover the 'institutional sclerosis' in most of the EEC countries has a lot to do with the fact that their governments do not take action of this kind.

The combination of subsidies and a failure to intervene has had a particularly mischievous effect at the level of the EEC,[14] from agrobusiness to coal, steel and nuclear energy to typical failures to intervene in the automobile and chemicals industries. All these industries which had been successful in the post-war cycle have become well organized at EEC level and are taking advantage of the political weakness of this quasi-state. In this sense the concept of 'Eurosclerosis' certainly has some justification, but not in the sense attributed to it by the supporters of *laissez-faire*.

The EEC countries provide material for a clearer illustration of what a distorted crisis mechanism is. Pressure for change is communicated too late; it is perceived only when greater flexibility elsewhere has already produced innovations. The process of problem-shelving has high social costs. At this stage the crisis itself tends to have only destructive effects. This means that the crisis that was postponed is not a factor of innovation and development.

I believe the long-wave theory to be an important one, because it is a theory of long-term thrusts for economic development which take effect through structural crises and fundamental innovations (G. Mensch). In this connection it is of interest that there is also a theory of long-term development thrusts in political science, or at least there are important points of departure for such a theory.

For example, Pye maintains that political systems are developing by overcoming crises of legitimation, participation, integration or distribution, and this at ever-higher stages.[15] In this theory the concept of 'political crisis of development' goes back to the psychoanalyst Erikson.[16] According to this view, political development or 'modernization' means the discontinuous enlargement and institutionalization of capabilities and capacities of the political system over time.

There are parallel concepts in marxist theory. The crisis does not simply reestablish the periodically disturbed unity of consumption and production. With the long-term accumulation of capital in the world market it also leads to the crisis-led formation of ever higher forms of intervention by the state.[17] Both these concepts could be interpreted to mean that successful crisis management by the state in long-term development thrusts becomes institutionalized at ever higher stages. As a rule this is accompanied by a more or less radical change of the élite, which springs from politicized crises. The upshot of all this is a concept of social and institutional innovation through crises.

Following Olson and others it can be presumed that in late phases of socioeconomic development this process can also be seriously distorted. It is not necessary to adduce the fate of absolutism or of large kingdoms like the Ottoman Empire or ancient China to attach importance to this question. In every case their decline was accompanied not only by unmanageability and incapacity for reform of an ossified power structure in the economy and the state, but also by the appearance of unfavourable foreign trade balances and of chronic state indebtedness.

A distorted crisis mechanism, a mechanism which only destroys without triggering any creative reaction, is the product of historically accumulated power whose privilege of not being compelled to be innovative becomes transmuted in time into inability to be innovative. It is a structure whose resources of power have made it comfortable, atrophying the flexibility engendered by necessity. Innovations are good for the processes of power formation, but power formation processes are not good for innovation. In the end they cause the production process to degenerate into a mere source of redistribution. That is when the concept of the 'rent-seeking society' gains relevance.[18]

Does not the dilemma of the aged and decrepit industrial system largely lie in the fact that during the present century more and more branches of industry have made use of the state and made their way to its feeding trough – often after having previously exhausted all the opportunities of market domination? And do not the innovation problems of many industrial countries, and the financial problems of their states, stem above all from the propensity of industrial power to do this? Is this not the 'system' worldwide?

We should be able to agree on the following basic structuralist critique of the rigidities of industrial countries. The market ought to be freed from usurpation by monopolies and the hegemony of traditional industries, most of which are particularly damaging to the environment, and brought back to an employment-effective creativity. The state should be freed from its involvements with powerful old industries and should make the transition from ineffectively intervening in details to truly influencing the ground rules, so that adaptability should keep pace with the need for change. At the same time the entire superstructure of the old industries should be renewed, to comply with the new standards and meet the requirements of openness.

How much has been done along these lines in the EEC countries? What part do the initiators of a changed course of development play there? What part do the advocates of appropriate technology play in the economy? What part do reformers play in the state? What role do the minorities carrying forward their critiques in society play? What part do the innovators play in science, and what contribution are they making to a process of renewal that will overcome the crisis?

A comprehensive process of innovation is more than the implementation of a standard range of technical inventions, the mere imitation of successful initiatives or the coopting of some innovators (e.g. by buying their companies). It is also more than promoting innovation through the old oligarchies. After all, 'innovator movements' (*Neurerbewegungen*) have existed in Eastern Europe as well for a long time as the demand for a 'scientific revolution'. The results are generally held to be unsatisfactory.

A radical process of innovation has to affect every part of the structure. It has to result in a fundamental improvement in the conditions for creativity and will bring forth its *own* innovations. The fact that large hierarchically centralized organizations also value innovations and are constantly offering 'something new' is no reason for entrusting this breakthrough to them.

Social innovations

I shall now try to illustrate from three sub-areas of social engineering the effects that a thoroughgoing process of innovation should produce. These are some of the priority areas for social innovations:

1   control and organization
2   information and training
3   motivation and acceptance.

For the reasons given earlier I attribute the contemporary structural crisis mainly to problems of guidance and control. International comparisons show that at the present time the known new scientific technologies are not by themselves the determinants of success. Rather, the deciding factor is better directive mechanisms. Because we have eyes only for the hardware we have failed to notice that if countries in Scandinavia or southeast Asia have put in place social innovations such as long-term planning which have demonstrated their value during the 1970s. This covert international competition for the effectiveness of directive mechanisms is of itself sufficient to ensure that *laissez-faire* strategies cannot do all that is required nowadays.

Both the traditional direction-setting institutions – the state and the market – are showing defects that have to be cured. State failure presupposes previous market failure. It has been shown in previous chapters that the market has manifest imperfections as a steering institution.

- It is often monopolistically dominated by old- established industries and hence is not an effective instrument to counter their inertia.
- It does give direction (by means of crises), but it does so too late, too harshly and with excessive social costs.
- It has at all times a medium-term outlook, that of the business cycle, and fails to meet the challenge of foreseeable future needs.
- It also fails to satisfy public interest requirements.

The state for its part exhibits substantial defects.

- It suffers from weakness in intervention described in detail earlier on.
- It too has a medium-term outlook, that of the election cycle.
- As understood in the Western democracies it takes the experience of the 'common man' as its standard.[19] However, there is an increasing number of experiences that should be avoided, from a third world war to disasters at chemicals plants or nuclear power stations. Such experiences must be forestalled by political means.

After all the foregoing, there is no need to add to the list. What is needed is consensual outline planning, which already exists in embryo. The planning must be consensual because that is the only way to include the concerns of the innovative and future-oriented minorities in the direction-setting process, and also because state-organized consensual processes are the best means of over-coming situations of political impotence, especially in times of crisis. It must be outline planning, as opposed to bureaucratic detailed planning, because the state certainly cannot replace the innovations of the decentralized protago-nists. The state can point them in the right direction, however – and as things are at present, this is more necessary than ever – but there must not be a controlling or sponsoring civil servant behind every researcher and engineer; the state is not competent to prescribe the 'right' technology in detail.

The people best fitted to assess the results of technology are the technicians and producers themselves – provided that they are working within the right ground rules. The state has a duty to keep these rules constantly under develop-ment in the light of the latest findings as to the problems. Technical risks must be internalized and converted into economic risks, which are foreseeable right from the research stage. This process must include, in the case of serious risks, an absolute prohibition under severe and credible penalties. In the case of long-term risks, deterrent taxation or fees increasing over time should often be suffi-cient to persuade those concerned to change to more appropriate technologies.

The creation of bureaucratic super-control organizations cannot be the answer to today's formidable problems of control. Experience has already taught us that the monitors and the monitored will soon become accomplices as long as the monitors do not have an interest of their own in the matter – which, after all, those affected and the potential victims have.

The crucial requirement with regard to institutional innovation is that centralization and division of labour must give way to decentralization and more complex units. This is the goal that is so easy to discern and so hard to achieve.

We have the technologies needed for improving the information situation. But what of the information itself, and the institutions that are to produce and distribute it, for despite all reforms higher education furnishes a model example of 'institutional sclerosis'? The favoured position of not having to be innovative is palpably evident at the universities. Not only do the academic institutions suffer from the circumstance that old professors teach there what other old professors taught them, but also education is based on the existing scientific, social and intellectual techniques and refers to them – but the unsuitability of these techniques is precisely the problem. And whereas the problems of industrial society lie increasingly in complex interdependence situations, we find that the academic structures are extremely specialized with a strong tendency to neglect the cross-linking of their knowledge.

Our future is not written in the stars, but the traditional conduct of academe bids fair to drown the fateful questions of society in a babble of astrologists, each one talking about a different star. In other words the extent and randomness of atomized specialization are conducive to speculative mystification.

As everywhere else in capitalism, so in the information sector there is poverty in the midst of plenty. Whole disciplines are underdeveloped; they include futurology, the environmental sciences, epidemiology, research aimed at problem-solving social discoveries and organizational sciences dealing with enhancing the effectiveness of democratic, participative and decentralized processes (democracy stimulates motivation – but only if it is sufficiently effective).

It is hard to understand why the Europe of the EEC obtains the greater part of its 'cultural products' from the United States. Even greater is the dependence on American data banks and research institutes of every kind. In return the West Europeans supply steel to the United States – highly subsidized steel. We also need improved intellectual techniques and information structures which would counteract the processes of self-deception conducive to the tank syndrome of superindustrialism.

In addition to the control and information dilemmas, thoroughgoing innovations in society should also counter the motivation and acceptance dilemma of traditional industrialism. Motivation is not achieved by propaganda and indoctrination, as the tank mentality suggests. The frequently bewailed absence of motivation to achieve in manufacturing and in educational institutions is due to processes of alienation caused by the structures. It must surely be a cause of shame in Europe with its democratic tradition when even late feudal Japan has found a better solution to the problem of motivation. A glance at indigenous alternative enterprises, or at experiments at Volvo, where participative structures are being tried out should be sufficient.

The problem of acceptance likewise affects consumers of products and of the damaging consequences of the industrial system. Many branches of industry – most recently the asbestos industry – have had to learn that public opinion is quite capable of producing effects in economics, and citizens are devoting more and more time to criticism. Moreover, problems of acceptance also arise in connection with the meaning of work. Higher product quality standards must also be set; frequently these are achieved by newcomers rather than by the old industries.

It goes without saying that the legitimacy of state activities is part of the acceptance problem. Governments may rely on the media for support, but citizens become aware of state failure through the facts as well.

Even more than in the sphere of science and technology, new social techniques are not so much a question of discoveries as of innovations – of inventions which should be implemented against privileges and established positions of power. Schumpeter believes that crisis in a technologically outmoded economy sets up 'creative destruction'.[20] Can there also be creative destruction of incrusted power relationships?

10 State Failure in Scientific Socialism

The problems of control and innovation arising in developed industrialism already discussed can be further illustrated from its communist variant. The gigantomania of superindustry, the cult of quantitative growth, the weight-of-metal bias of production, squandering of resources and environmental problems, centralization with division of labour and the tank syndrome are particularly marked in communism. It can scarcely be credibly denied that hierarchical centralism in the bureaucracy and industry have inhibited development. Eastern European countries suggest more than anything else that the answer to the problems involved in steering superindustries is not to be found in super-bureaucracies. They also point to the problems of government in a system that cripples the market.

The communist countries of Eastern Europe are only an extreme example of the problems besetting *all* industrialized countries, however, and this leaves little room for smug superiority in the West. I would even contend that part of Eastern Europe's problems, both economic and environmental, arises from extensive imitation of Western industrialism, although the amalgam of super-industrialism and authoritarian rule creates additional problems.

We shall not be able to draw any lessons from what has happened in these countries if we approach them in a spirit of self-congratulation and fail to see what are their specific possibilities, some of which have not been exploited.[1]

Advantages of the system

At first glance the Soviet-type socialist countries have considerable room for manoeuvre. They appear to be very well placed for moulding the future and making the public interest prevail.

- Annual, medium-term and in some cases longer-term plans are drawn up with the formal broad participation of all parties that have an important interest.
- All public interests considered appropriate can be comprehensively represented in the organization and information system.
- There is no mass unemployment, so often used as a pretext for perpetuating unwanted production under capitalism.
- Capital is owned by the nation. Political pressures involving the threat to take capital elsewhere, or not to invest, have no place.
- The system does not depend on wasteful consumption for growth, and waste through overproduction is not a frequent occurrence.
- There is a significantly lower level of social problems such as criminality than under capitalism.
- In many areas, excluding the power centres, there is a comparatively marked equality of opportunity.
- The educational system is geared to the needs of society, and the problem of lack of skills seems to be less acute than in most Western countries.

Even if we use the tests applied in the main part of this book, namely health or environmental protection or structural policy, a very differentiated picture emerges.

The health system in East Germany, for example, does well in international comparisons with regard to the fall in infant mortality for instance, or general areas of preventive medicine, which has a strong component of social medicine and penetrates even the factories.

With regard to the environment the long tradition of nature protection, which goes back to Lenin, and the care of historical urban architecture are also worthy of mention.

With regard to clean air maintenance, the state intervened in a big way under Kruschev (who incidentally was an opponent of private mass motorization)[2] when the situation became acute in Moscow. After 1956 the worst air polluters in the city were converted from coal to oil or gas, and industrial undertakings were later moved away from the city. Similarly radical measures were taken in Shanghai under Mao Tse-tung.[3]

Eastern Europe is less urbanized and motorized and has less private consumption of goods than the West, all of which improves the prospects for protection of the environment and of health.

Protection of the environment was enshrined in the constitution of East Germany as early as 1968, and it was the second country in Europe (after Sweden) to pass a comprehensive law on protection of the environment (the Land Culture Law of 1970). Until the oil crisis struck, improvements were also made in the area of water and air pollution.

Disadvantages of the system

Yet it is precisely with regard to environmental and health protection that the difficulties confronting protection interests of this kind can be illustrated. The reactor disaster at Chernobyl was an extreme example, far worse than similar incidents at Harrisburg and Windscale. We are very conscious of all aspects of this occurrence, and I shall therefore mention some other facts.

Life expectancy in the countries of Eastern Europe is very low compared with that in other industrial countries. In 1987 it was between 68 years (in the Soviet Union) and 71 (in East Germany). Nowadays those values are exceeded in many marginal countries such as Costa Rica, Hong Kong and even Cuba. In most of the industrial countries life expectancy is now between 76 years (in West Germany) and 79 (in Japan).[4]

Sulphur dioxide pollution per head of the population is the highest in East Germany and Czechoslovakia out of industrial countries, and it is also comparatively high in Poland[5] and Hungary.[6] In this connection the lack of desulphurization equipment on large coal-fired power stations constitutes a special problem. There are in East Germany and Czechoslovakia – on both sides of the Ore Mountains, whose problems have been well known for the past 25 years – lignite-fired power stations, every one of which emits as much sulphur dioxide into the air as the whole of Austria.[7] In so far as passably accurate measurements exist – most of them made during the 1970s – the air pollution in densely populated areas of Eastern Europe is high, and internationally most comparable with those of some large cities in southern Europe.[8]

The connection between air pollution, sickness and life expectancy in Eastern Europe is well known. At any rate in East Germany it was discovered that by reducing emissions of noxious substances in the worst-affected areas by half it was possible to increase life expectancy by about four years, to reduce malignant growths in the air passages by a quarter and to decrease heart and circulatory illnesseses by 10–15 per cent.[9]

As under capitalism, it costs more not to prevent damage to the environment than to prevent it. In the USSR the cost of damage caused by water pollution alone amounted to between 4,000 million and 6,000 million roubles in 1980, which is two or three times as much as the total invested in protection of the environment in the country in that year.[10]

Despite this the plans were conducive to contrary developments, and after a spate of environmental protection in the early 1970s such investments decreased (in East Germany) or at any rate remained unchanged (in the USSR), whilst private mass motorization was promoted so that it rose steeply at the same time. East Germany forms an exception with regard to road freight traffic, which was systematically reduced in favour of rail freight after the second oil crisis in 1979, falling by 28 per cent by 1987.[11]

Another setback was the increasing industrialization of agriculture, which took the form of extreme division of labour and centralization with a constant increase in the use of machinery and chemicals that still failed to produce sufficient food. The intensive use of labour also reflected badly on health policy. Because labour is so cheap, it was not replaced by machinery where this would have been preferable.

Lastly, the tendency for industry to be concentrated in large centres of population, a tendency encouraged by the state's 'territorial planning', was ill-conceived. As early as 1976 a standard East German publication stated that the general development led to 'a trend to further concentration of the population in large housing estates . . . this is in line with the international trend to the growth of cities'.[12] At that time this trend had long since been reversed in the United States and elsewhere.

However, the failure of the state with regard to health and environmental policy in the communist countries of Eastern Europe is connected above all with the way industries are run. The ruling pattern of industrialization is that of an even more extreme centralized division of labour than that once practised in the West. One of the consequences is an enormous need for freight transport. Moreover, ever since Stalin the pattern of industrialization has shown a bias towards heavy industry, which is still very marked compared with other countries notwithstanding the efforts that have been made since 1953 to promote light industry.

Above all, however, industry plays a dominant role in the macroeconomic planning aims. A large part of the services sector is left out of the national accounts as 'unproductive' in the statistics of the overall economy. This goes back to Marx and Lenin and leads us into an ideological depth dimension of the problems of Eastern Europe with respect to economic and environmental problems that certainly cannot be disregarded. I maintain that structural change in the direction of post-industrialism has been obstructed for ideological reasons as well.

In any event the most important task of innovation facing the economies of Eastern Europe is that of shedding the incubus of heavy industry. This is urgent both for economic and ecological reasons. Quite contrary to capitalist industry, there is in the Eastern economic community of Comecon a strong tendency to wastefulness at *corporate* level. Whereas under capitalism extravagance is mainly connected with private consumption, in the Eastern countries enterprises waste materials and energy. Specific resource consumption is inordinately high. This was originally caused by the market failure of a price system which undervalued factors of production of this kind. It became a problem when the world prices of raw materials rose – and protection of the environment became an issue.

What difference has state planning made since the early 1970s in the light of this challenge?

The previously mentioned study made by Berlin Free University on relieving stress on the environment through economic structural change indicates that Czechoslovakia and East Germany had the highest average per capita use of energy and raw steel, cement and weight of goods transported by rail and road. Whilst structural pressure caused by these factors was decreasing in many Western countries, it increased during the 1970s almost everywhere in Eastern Europe. This too shows a parallel with the capitalist countries in southern Europe.

All in all, the dogged persistance of the old-fashioned industrial trend is astonishing. Here too East Germany is an exception, for there a distinct structural change has been discernible since 1979. Consumption of raw steel and cement have slightly decreased, and there was only a slight increase in primary energy consumption, whilst there was a 16 per cent decrease in the weight of goods transported by road and rail between 1980 and 1987.[13]

These are quite considerable effects of state intervention. But why do they appear so late? And why are they only just appearing in other countries in the communist camp? Why have perceptions about environmental protection, 'materials economy', 'intensification' and the 'scientific revolution' with which they are bound up not taken more effect? Why have the advantages of the system borne so little fruit? What are the causes of the 'inertia, stagnation and conservatism' of which Gorbachev has spoken?[14]

The answer is to be found principally in the following *disadvantages* of the system:

1 a machinery of planning that does not concentrate on prospects of smooth development and influencing the basic conditions but is constantly becoming enmeshed in production details;
2 a rigid pricing system which fails to supply important information;
3 an orientation of production and motivation which is determined from the top downwards and leads to a lack of flexibility with regard to consumers, citizens or new requirements;
4 a predominance of plant profitability calculations under the rigid planning mechanism, reinforced by problems on the world market, e.g. to invest in environmental protection would worsen the important economic 'indices' of the plant;
5 over-representation of the powerful traditional industries in the planning hierarchy, the main lobbyist for each industry being the responsible minister for the industry with his bureaucracy of specialists in a narrow range of products (vertical concentration is the rule as opposed to horizontally concentrated conglomerates with their greater flexibility);

6 disregard of the economic potential of information and services and their potential for innovation (the myth of industry);
7 all kinds of bureaucratic excesses connected with the strong position held by the security forces;
8 market failure with reference to independent technological creativity, and environmental problems not even being paid for via an ecological industry (however inadequate the add-on damage-reducing technology of such an industry may be judged to be);
9 a mania for secrecy and palliation, typical of oligarchic structures, resulting in self-deception, information gaps and inadequate delayed reactions to problems;
10 absence of innovative thrust due to the effects of deep-seated defects, a lack of organizational freedom and legal rights, and insufficient media support for interests that run counter to the prevailing trend of super-industry making inertia endemic, as it does elsewhere in the world;
11 lack of clear demarcation of spheres of responsibility, a propensity to pass the buck and people's being relieved of responsibility through centralized division of labour (since nearly everything is decided at the centre, responsibility can be delegated 'upwards' to the heart's content);
12 and not least, the weak position of the communes and regions, which is fraught with consequences.

But there is even a further dimension to these barriers to innovation, which we shall now address.

The 'international trend' as a yardstick

Anybody looking into the effectiveness of the steering mechanisms of the communist planning system in Eastern Europe could easily fall into the error of neglecting its philosophy of government. Many of the trends described were deliberately chosen in order to 'make up lost ground' or 'catch up with the international trend'.

Otto Kirchheimer once distinguished several stages of 'revolutionary break-throughs'.[15] His criterion was how far in each case the 'restrictive conditions' of the old society were overcome. A simple change of personnel or just breaching constitutional structures did not amount to the depth dimension of a revolution, which also includes the whole system of property relationships. The Russian revolution of 1917 was a complete revolution on this interpretation.

Mao Tse-tung discovered yet another depth dimension – that of culture – and if we equate this with the concept of 'political culture' due to Almond and

Verba, it can easily be observed that the political culture of Tsarist Russia was not completely superseded any more than, let us say, the political culture of the old Poland or that of Prussia was superseded in the German Democratic Republic. Traditions of the education of children, man–woman relationships or attitudes to the 'authorities' have proved to be astonishingly persistent under the new conditions. In this they strongly resemble the traditions of Confucianism in China which so upset Mao. From the viewpoint of certain radically democratic ideas of marxism, these were undoubtedly 'restrictive conditions'.

The same is true of the centralism of the state. But it is crucially true of the method of production – the material and social technology of the capitalist industrial production system. Marx was concerned with the production relationships, the exploitation of wage labour by an ever-decreasing number of capitalists. What might be called the 'technological culture' of industrial capitalism he sometimes criticized in a completely visionary manner: 'Capitalist production develops technology, and the combining together of the various processes into a social whole, only by sapping the original sources of all wealth – the soil and the labourer.'[16] But he was just as fascinated by the technology of developed capitalism. That at least was not the object of his revolutionary hopes.

This was even clearer in the case of Lenin. The ambivalence of endeavouring to bring in a totally different order of society whilst taking the techniques of capitalism as a model goes back to him, and what he had in mind was the material and social technology of the 'most progressive capitalist countries', from assembly line production to large centralized organizations practising strict division of labour. The immediate justification for this was the objective of catching up, but perhaps the causes lie deeper. This imitative attitude towards the West was shown even by Peter the Great. And imitation is hierarchical centralism's substitute for innovation. Failure to breach the political culture of Tsarism, coupled with the lack of an indigenous technological culture, has had consequences for the Soviet system that have determined its course of development. The authoritarian traditions encouraged the basic attitude of imitation, and Lenin's understanding of technology gave the direction. The model for the *method* of production was, and still is, the megamachine of capitalist large-scale industry.

Integration into the capitalist world market

Against this background it is rather surprising that it took the communist countries until the 1960s to draw the full conclusions from this situation and become once more integrated into the capitalist world market.[17] There were two significant reasons for this step – and a further possible important reason was missing. The countries of Eastern Europe have a sufficiency of raw materials. Hence, unlike countries such as West Germany, they were not compelled to take part in the world market by a lack of raw materials.

The two reasons are (a) that agricultural production was insufficient, even in the former 'granaries' of Eastern Europe, necessitating imports from the developed capitalist countries, as only the latter were net exporters of agricultural products, and (b) 'technological backwardness'.

However, both these reasons have a lot to do with the fact that the state socialist countries of Eastern Europe have become exponents of hierarchical centralism. Basically they tried to overcome problems of innovation, motivation and inefficiencies by taking the indirect route of the world market. They hoped also that the legitimation problems of the authoritarian structure would be diminished in this way.

Instead of creating social structures favourable to innovation, they relied on the innovations of the West. Instead of themselves supplying their domestic market with attractive goods, they relied upon the attraction of Western products. Instead of strengthening the popular base of the system through more open participative structures they relied on legitimation through the blessings of intensive industrial growth. The low motivation to produce and develop new ideas, which is the problem of all hierarchical superstructures, can be regarded as the cardinal problem. Three phases can be distinguished for the Soviet-type socialist countries with respect to basic motivations.

In the first phase there was the *élan* of those who were for the first time the favoured ones and the ideological motivation of people with plenty of opportunity to apply their ideas who were generally rewarded with swift promotion. During the first phase authoritarian patterns of leadership played a role, but did not become crucially important until the spontaneous motivations had died down or even became politically suspect, as happened in the Stalin era. In this second phase the totalitarian compulsion received an oppressive overemphasis.

However, an industrial system cannot remain successful when subjected to centralized compulsion. Therefore in the post-Stalin era, under the influence of the crisis of growth, 'material interest' was increasingly declared to be the 'economic lever'. If performance is to be stimulated through higher bonuses and similar incentives, however, the consumer goods which alone make the possession of money attractive must be made available, and as the level of production rises so the level of the consumer goods must also rise attractively. Thus one constraining factor followed another until finally there remained so little room for political manoeuvre that private motoring, which had little to do with socialism, had to be facilitated by the costly import of cars from the West.

Material interests and the consumerism associated with them always become preponderant in production to the extent that they serve to compensate for alienated meaningless circumstances. Industrial psychologists had already discovered this in the 1930s. How to create motivation through more self-realization in production is a question which all hierarchical centralized systems have to face. The socialist industrial system should have been especially familiar with it. At all events the price of extensive reorientation towards the world market was high, for the world market is a capitalist institution which will only work satisfactorily according to the rules of capitalism. Consequently the communist countries were at first competing in this institution only like large enterprises with an internal structure that was alien to the market system. Gradually, however, the internal structures of these countries also began to be brought into line with the imperatives of the world market. The argument that 'protection of the environment hampers competitiveness' was symptomatic of this situation.

Poland paid the highest price for this kind of integration into the world market; under Gierek the country had entered capitalist terrain with a special euphoria. They wanted to manufacture the products of Western technology (e.g. of Fiat) on the favourable conditions of their own system and then sell them at low prices to Western customers. The investment was paid for with loans from Western banks. The Polish products were indeed cheaper, but their quality was regarded as unsatisfactory. Consequently Poland (like Romania) remained heavily in debt to the West – more seriously than other countries in Eastern Europe. Yet most of the Comecon countries were able to pay off their indebtedness more quickly than budgetary deficits were reduced in Western countries.

Another consequence of integration into the world market was the tremendous increase in state expenditures during the 1970s. Export subsidies and all manner of price supports proliferated – whilst savings were made on protection of the environment.

Naturally the basis of socialist identity and legitimation in these countries suffered in the process, for basically capitalism was declared to be the highest stage of socialism. In my view an unmistakable pointer to this loss of political identity is the fact that during the 1950s and 1960s the opposition in Eastern Europe appealed to Marx and Engels (the non-Soviet tradition of marxism), whereas later on they relied on the Western concept of human rights.

Barriers to innovation

There were already economic discussions in the Soviet Union and in East Germany in the early 1970s on the theme that 'materials economy' was the best way to protect the environment.[18] In Eastern Europe as a whole they have borne remarkably little fruit until very recently. For a long time the planning hierarchy distanced itself from such discussions, and the 'tonnes ideology' remained obstinately in vogue.

By contrast, the debate on decentralization in Hungary did produce effects. In 1982 Janos Kornai published an investigation into how the economic success of enterprises compared with their size.[19] The study showed conclusively that profitability decreased sharply with size. This finding would have caused no surprise in the West, where it would have reinforced the bicycle syndrome. Nor is it surprising that such a conclusion was drawn in Hungary, a small country, before it became apparent to the other members of the bloc, but it resulted in the breakup of large enterprises into much smaller units.

Equally interesting in this connection was a debate in East Germany on the problems connected with innovation and the structural 'barriers' to technological 'creativity'. A paper given by Heinz-Dieter Haustein of the 'Bruno Leuschner College of Economics' in East Berlin entitled 'Creativity and innovation on the way to the 21st century'[20] deserves special mention here.

Quite in the spirit of Schumpeter or Gerhard Mensch he takes as his starting point long-term 'cycles of innovation' proceeding from 'basic innovation' via 'improvement innovations' to the final 'saturation trend'. His paper is noteworthy because he also discusses the social context of innovative thrusts, suggesting that these should 'come from the whole life rhythm of a society, from its inner movement against phenomena of boredom, self-satisfaction, arrogance, organizational rigidity and unwillingness to learn. This is the real challenge of the future, which countries with differing social orders must face.'[21]

One of the factors he regards as critical is the 'relationship between creativity and routine'. 'All élitist ideologies start with the assumption that creativity is the privilege of élites at the top.' But 'who then is going to bring forth technical progress with its myriad manifestations?'[22] The 'barriers' to innovation are illustrated in the striking table 11.

Haustein showed empirically that a cyclic process of innovations is discernible in East Germany as well. His graph of the development of benefits from innovative proposals had a peak at the end of the 1960s, after which it fell continuously until 1980. This trend could also be interpreted as showing that the innovation potential of the old superindustrial structure has been exhausted.

Table 11   Constraints on creativity during its formative and fruition phases

	Barriers			
	Level and growth of productive forces	Economic relations and interests	Institutions	Intellectual and ideological factors
Formation of creative personalities	Lack of nourishment	No economic interest in creative persons	Inadequate educational system; illiteracy	Elitist theories and ideologies
Creative period	Inadequate material conditions; too little leisure	Economic incentives for 'brain drain' and frustration. Unemployment	Social anti-creative aims and tasks of institutions. Organizations in saturation phase	Attitude against creative people; uncreative atmosphere; anxiety for the future; alienation
Period of performance	Material constraints	Insufficient incentive to innovation, excessive division of labour; Unemployment	Institutional constraints	No understanding between R & D and production

Source: Heinz-Dieter Haustein, 1983

Conclusion: are politics impotent?

A Western observer may find it difficult to talk about the impotence of politics in the socialist countries of Eastern Europe (before 1989). We had the picture of the 'total state' whose 'omnipotence' was manifest, and the state did indeed have a great deal of power to reinforce trends or to stabilize structures in these countries. Nevertheless I maintain that it was precisely this quantitatively total power structure in the state that made it a colossus with feet of clay. If politics are regarded as strategy, as a process of laying down ground rules and of decision-making, in any event as the sum of measures against the prevailing trend, there is reason for holding this opinion.

For in those countries too the prevailing trend was the momentum of prevailing circumstances. Neither the public interest, the interests of affected people, nor the interests of the future was more strongly organized than under the market economy system, and as businesses became more independent their particularist interest tended to be strengthened without any improvement worth mentioning in the ability of the state to take independent decisions.

The socialist states in Eastern Europe were not the prey of organized lobby power and the redistributive processes associated with the old large-scale industries to the extent that they are in the West. In Eastern Europe industry ranked *after* the bureaucracy; in many cases the bureaucracy set it up. But this very fact created special problems connected with the close interlinking of bureaucracy and industry, which is a dangerous situation under capitalism as well. The large industries did not constantly have to get the state on their side, using whatever means were available. Usually the state *was* on their side, because all the planning was carried out largely by the industrialists concerned and the ministry for that industry. Any conflicts between them were primarily conflicts about growth rates. Usually the state conducted veritable campaigns for scientific and technical progress, but such is the inertia of big industry that it may easily fail in its objective.

Modernization promoted by the state in Eastern Europe was very largely the modernization of existing industries, aimed at making them more efficient and internationally competitive. In countries such as East Germany progress has been made in some areas with innovative improvements carried out with assistance from the state. As in Western countries with a political preponderance of traditional branches of industry, the main problem is the transfer of resources to new industries that do not yet exist, and for which therefore no ministerial lobby exists.

The task of industrial restructuring will be even more difficult than in Western countries.

The planning concept of the Soviet Communist Party plan for the period 1986–2000 stated with some confidence: 'Industrial production is to be at least doubled. Heavy industry, the foundation of the country's industry, is to be constantly consolidated.' Nuclear energy was to be increased at least fivefold to sevenfold, and the chemical industry was also very important.[23] On the other hand, resource-saving was to become one of the principal means of meeting the growing needs of the economy: seventy to 80 per cent of the additional demand for fuels, energy, commodities and industrial raw materials must be met by this means.' 'More use must be made of non-traditional, renewable and secondary sources of energy.'[24] No doubt even more emphasis has been laid on these requirements after the Chernobyl catastrophe. The provision of services for the population is also to rise more than proportionately, but the USSR is very far from having a comprehensive strategy of tertiarization.

Viewed ecologically, these long-term plans envisage only a modest relaxation of environmental stress through technical and structural change, in relation to the growth of the economy. This makes traditional protection of the environment all the more urgent, yet only of late have the planners seemed to attribute more importance to it.[25] Therefore the problems of traditional industrialism are more likely to increase in the course of time.

The countries of Eastern Europe will have to develop a political and technical culture of their own and create the appropriate conditions for them in the social structure. As in Western industrialism it would be necessary to reduce the sizes and degree of interlocking between the bureaucracy and industry to dimensions which would leave sufficient scope to politics and allow the producers enough motivation.

That would be a task of radical innovation, to which the long-buried traditions of socialism could help point the way – the creation of a more decentralized system with strong local communities, with the producers (and the citizens) strongly motivated through effective participation, having a political centre whose primary task is to lay the ground rules, to organize consensual processes and to smooth out inequalities among the decentralized units.

There is a great danger that the industrial conservatism of the EC countries will again be strengthened through the imitation and importation by the East. But there might be the chance of a 'Third Way' 26) with social and technical innovations that provide better solutions for the next century. This way is much more difficult because it includes more than the restoration of human rights and a parliamentary democracy. The critical part along that way begins when the traditional bureaucratic-industrial policy networks prove to be resistant to a revolution in merely the sphere of political institutions.

11 Finale: In Praise of Smaller Units

Are our environmental problems, technical and military risks, mass unemployment and state indebtedness sequels to a degenerate industrial structure that has become unmanageable? Is the state a part of this problematic trend? What are the causes of the inability of politics to mitigate the crisis by taking decisions against the trend? Under what conditions can politics be reinvigorated to serve the community?

These are the questions we have addressed. When making a detailed critical analysis I have repeatedly suggested alternatives. The overall alternative is this: if power accumulation processes in course of time stand in the way of learning processes and innovations and if inability to innovate leads to crises and stagnation, these crises should be seized politically as an opportunity to dismantle the strongholds of power. Since power becomes insecure at times of crisis, this impotence of politics in promoting the common interest does not have to be the last word.

There are five ways in which power can be dismantled:

1 by decentralization
2 by countervailing power from above
3 by countervailing power from below
4 by countervailing power from outside
5 by countervailing power from within.

(1) *Decentralization* is the most important of these, because it is an improvement on the other possible means of dismantling power. 'Small is beautiful' is an old theme in political science. Two hundred and forty years ago Montesquieu praised the advantages of the small republic and described the optimum conditions for democratic politics:

> 'It is natural for a republic to have only a small territory . . . In an extensive republic there are men of large fortunes, and

consequently of less moderation; there are trusts too considerable to be placed in any single subject; he has interests of his own . . . In an extensive republic the public good is sacrificed to a thousand private views; it is subordinate to exceptions, and depends on accidents. In a small one, the interest of the republic is easier perceived, better understood, and more within the reach of every citizen; abuses have less extent, and of course are less protected.'[1]

Even today small countries have many advantages in common[2] that distinguish them from the Great Powers and from countries with large concentrations of power and capital. It is the smaller industrialized countries which on average have a higher life expectancy. Most of them have a comparatively high per capita standard of living, and they generally spend less on armaments. It is the great countries of the world who are responsible for most of the military interventions and who also suffer the biggest nuclear accidents. Even within national states the smaller units at the lower levels appear to be more efficient and effective than the centres. However, naive concepts of decentralization are to be avoided.

Effective decentralization depends on effective centres, though the centres are effective only if they confine themselves to overall compensatory and coordination functions. Material discrepancies between rich and poor regions and localities have to be ironed out if ruinous competition between them is to be avoided and work is not constantly to flow to the best-placed localities in the capital. All the efforts to impose conditions upon the worldwide economy that are in line with local public interests have to be coordinated. The impotence of politics in the industrial system will be lessened to the extent that its local base is materially strengthened and its overall coordination is improved.

(2) Countervailing power from above is state power. It has already been emphasized that industrial superpower cannot be controlled by the bureaucratic superpower of the state; the two forms of power are too similar to one another and they too easily become allied. In the last resort the only remedy is to dismantle industrial power. This could be achieved by restricting the amount of public money flowing into industry's coffers.

However, politics can also improve its position with regard to legitimation. It can refuse to allow the present decision-takers to effect legitimation, adopt a critical stance itself and disclose the real seats of responsibility. It can improve its position by organizing consensual processes, seeking new allies and broadening its political base. Politics can also improve its position on the world market by lessening the weight of competition pressing upon it through international agreements. International agreements to end competitive subsidization, to unify tax policies regarding corporations or for preventive health protection are examples of what could be done.

Countervailing political power from above is provided by consensual planning, which was dealt with in chapter 9. In this situation politics also improves its position because it concentrates on the overall ground rules and focuses on general objectives instead of prescribing technical means in detail. This 'economy' of central government (or international) intervention would also include the ability of the subordinate units not only to take over detailed implementation but also to have some room for discretionary action in the public interest. Local authorities, for example, which are in a position to improve upon the minimum standards imposed by higher authority offer more protection for the citizen, besides being a factor in innovation, as the example of Japan has shown.

(3) Politics from above can increase its independence by institutionally strengthening the countervailing power from below. This has to do with what was described in chapter 2 as the third layer of control besides the state and the market, namely intervention by those affected. In contrast with the small number of officials who are supposed to monitor a subsector of the economy for compliance with standards, citizens on the receiving end may have a genuine and lively interest in doing the monitoring. The risk of their becoming connivers with the questionable process is minimal. The politically and organizationally underprivileged position of people in need of protection who are not engaged in industry or commerce must be ended as far as possible. This applies to the material, legal and publicity aspects. The complaints procedure must be improved rather than restricted, and environmental protection, tenants' and other public interests must be represented on the boards of radio and television companies. After the experiences of the last ten years, anybody who weakens this level of control should not be surprised if a trend to stagnation sets in.

(4) Countervailing power from outside should be created by the market, according to traditional thinking, but for this to happen there must exist a cartel policy worthy of the name. Countervailing power of this sort could also be created by potential innovators in communications and science.

(5) Countervailing power from within could also place a curb on the powers of hierarchized centralism. This applies to rights of participation, which always provide the opportunity of raising motivation, and this in turn favours innovation. However, here too traditional ideas should be viewed with caution. Conventional codetermination, even at the universities during the 1970s, has not enhanced the effectiveness and motivation of those taking part sufficiently to be regarded as the last word on the subject. In this very area social discoveries and further developments are needed; the effects are more important than the formal structures.

Therefore a policy in the public interest is not fated to suffer the impotence described in this book, however heavily the structures bear down. The inertial drift of the giants of superindustrialism (and the masculine bias towards a power-oriented latently aggressive social and physical technology auto-nomized in them) harbour such formidable risks that every effort must be made to strengthen the power of politics.

Many detailed proposals for reversing state failure can be made, ranging from the planned utilization of the gratis effects of structural change, ecological modernization, the internalization of costs and risks, changes in the tax system discouraging resource consumption and encouraging labour, to the reform of the public service and its centralist income privileges. Many reforms that would free the state from the compulsion to growth can also be envisaged.

However, there is one problem central to all this. It is the power strata of a rigid hierarchical centralism in industry and the bureaucracy that has become sclerotic. If these power strata are not dismantled or neutralized they will become a millstone round the necks of the industrial countries which they have rendered incapable of reform.

If my experience is any guide, it is difficult to imagine the necessary changes taking place unless politics is strengthened from below, for the task of innovation would be too formidable. There is no public body that can relieve citizens of this task.

Methodological Appendix: Political Science as Realistic Analysis

Difficulties

Political science is a difficult subject. The problem begins with the abstractness of its subject matter. Although human beings do not differ much in physical strength, there are rulers and the ruled, but this relationship is as abstract as that to which it gives rise.

The state is just as abstract, and it is of little use for the citizen to think of the state as a father figure, just because that is a more familiar idea from childhood. What looks to the uninitiated like a father figure is more likely to be seen by the analyst as a large number of protagonists pulling in different directions. We need only think about the competition between widely differing bureaucracies for shares of the annual tax revenue. Thus it is not even clear whether the concept of the state refers to something that can be regarded as an acting subject, and to say that it can also be defined as the legitimate monopoly of decisions binding upon all citizens and as the bodies correspondingly charged with formulating and executing the will of the nation does not help much.

Nowhere is the abstractness of political entities better illustrated than by what we nowadays call the world market, which is deciding more and more, yet has no identifiable centres of decision. Its structure is highly abstract, but it has a very real effect on nations, regions or municipalities.

A further difficulty with political science arises precisely from this abstractness of its subject matter. Words like freedom, democracy, socialism, crisis and industrial society do not describe any objects or processes which we meet in everyday life. It would be truer to say that the object they indicate arises only from a concrete concept (or from its definition). The subject-matter of political science is constituted by its concepts. Consequently a distinction has to be made between word, concept and entity; words from the arsenal of political language (like freedom, democracy etc.) become a problem owing to the differing content attributed to them from time to time. And each of these differing concepts refers to other entities. When a communist talks about 'democratic countries' he means different countries from those to which a liberal would apply the term. The difference lies in the concept. Words in political language sound unambiguous, as if we have only to think about them long enough to grasp exactly what they stand for (like freedom or the state). Thomas Hobbes recognized that this is a false conclusion when he wrote: 'For words are wise men's counters, they do but reckon by them: but they are the money of fools.'[1]

This leads to the third difficulty for a scientific observation of politics, namely the problem of partiality and objectivity.

Politics is not only legitimate participation in socially binding decisions. It also bears the imprint of opposing interests and value judgements. A science like political science can only with difficulty be kept clear of these contradictions. Indeed, it is questionable whether there is any point in keeping it clear of them.

The problem of bias arises at two levels: (a) the normative level of valuation and volition and (b) the descriptive level of perception.[2] At both levels there is the problem of the 'standpoint-conditioning' of thinking. It is not only that the same word may evoke different objects because of differing connotations. Perhaps even more frequently the same object viewed through the lenses of differing (standpoint-conditioned) concepts can be seen differently. If I look at West Germany under the standpoint-conditioned concept of 'democracy', I see something different about it (quite objectively) from what is seen by somebody looking at the same object through the lense of the standpoint-conditioned concept of capitalism. The concept of the industrial society (which concentrates on the mode of production) again offers a different perspective and is based on different experiences.

These viewpoints are standpoint conditioned and one sided, but they do not exclude objectivity. Even a one-sided press photograph is objective, if it is not a fake.

The problem of partiality is therefore not its inability to be objective, but its particularity and the one-sidedness of its concepts. Thus, to pursue the analogy, it relates to more than one photograph, to photographs taken from different standpoints. Karl Mannheim asked in 1929 with reference to this problem: 'Is politics as a science possible?[3] He refers his theory of the social standpoint-conditioned nature of thinking to the political standpoints as well. For him too the problem is not that of objectivity but that of the 'particular *aspect structures*'. He believes the partisan viewpoint to be relevant, because it has not arisen by chance and is not random. He sees the problem of political science as residing in bringing the particularity of standpoint-conditioned viewpoints into a synthesis:

> Not only the necessary partisan character of every form of political knowledge is recognized, but also the peculiar character of each variety. It has become incontrovertibly clear today that all knowledge which is either political or which involves a world-view, is inevitably partisan. The fragmentary character of all knowledge is clearly recognizable. But this implies the possibility of an integration of many mutually complementary points of view into a comprehensive whole.
>
> Just because today we are in a position to see with increasing clarity that mutually opposing views and theories are not infinite in number and are not products of arbitrary will but are mutually complementary . . . politics as a science is for the first time possible.[4]

In the light of the lost wholeness of the developed industrial societies and the apparent chaos of partisan interpretations, this is an extremely important pronouncement.

We can at any rate take note that the particularity and one-sidedness of political viewpoints is not an insoluble dilemma, that the analytical fruitfulness of differing standpoint-conditioned aspect structures can certainly be examined with scientific independence and probity without the examiner's giving up his own standpoint. Partisanship can be combined with objectivity. Taking sides is not an arbitrary activity; it relates to vitally important points of conflict in society. It has at least this advantage over classroom learning.

However, the political positions, aims and values themselves constitute a problem of equal magnitude for scientific political analysis. For Mannheim too the dilemma was that science can make verifiable pronouncements only about facts and not about value judgements. Agreement can be reached as to the actual existence of facts, but not as to the correctness of standards. Yet political science, with the same justification as, say, economic science, is essentially an advisory science which not only describes empirically but also makes recommendations. It is impossible to see why political value judgements and decisions on aims should not also form the subject matter of this science. To make it a no-go area for scientific theory is simply to accept the monopoly of non-scientific value judgements, which is certainly not a value-free position.

In the last resort there are three ways in which science can be related to the values and standards ruling in a society. It can (a) *actively* support or even technologically reinforce them (just as fast breeder technology or the strategic defense initiative *de facto* radicalize existing value judgements), (b) *passively* support ruling values, as suggested by a value-neutral attitude, (c) make reasoned criticisms and propose changes. In times of social change such as the present a society's capacity for innovation will depend to a large extent on whether science adopts position (c).

It is true that values and standards cannot be given the force of obligation by scientific means, but they can be generalized by consensual methods and practices. What are involved are the rules of full and fair discussion of values or objectives – with a discourse free from domination or deception as an ideal model.[5]

In science and politics, consensual mechanisms for elaborating thoroughly discussed value and purpose objectives have become increasingly important. It seems as if the creativity of the industrial societies depends increasingly on them. In any event such a consensual principle does not abdicate because there is a plurality of standards and values. It is concerned with rational goal-setting, and it gives innovative minority positions a stronger say in matters than does the conventional majority model, or sterile thinking in categories of pluralistic incompatibilities.

The last obstacle to the analysis of political realities we mention is the 'dilemma between accuracy and relevance'.[6] Political science suffers particularly from the fact that with the best will in the world the most important parts of its subject matter are not susceptible to exact measurement. This is true of the analysis of power or of special interests, and of the analysis of central interdependences. Anybody who wants to be a 'good scientist' in the sense of making exact measurements would do well to choose another discipline. Yet these are precisely the matters that are increasingly acquiring vital importance for the developed industrial countries. Anyhow, surrender is not an option here either. The criterion of scientific plausibility does not satisfy the requirements of rigorous measurement technology, but in connection with the analysis of undeniable problems it is an acceptable standard.

Political science is, then, a difficult science. Yet there is not the slightest reason for it to accept the defensive attitude which it is repeatedly urged to adopt in society.

Two world views of the social sciences

The distinction in social science between idealism and realism, or even materialism, is an old but important one. So those who, like me, advocate a realist analysis of the state distance themselves from forms of idealist analysis. This discrimination has consequences, and a few words of explanation are necessary.

In the idealist view of the state and society, ideas and those who subscribe to them play a decisive role. Individual agents act in accordance with ideas and value judgements. History is the sum of these actions, and society is the sum of the 'relations' of these individuals to one another. Standards and values play an independent role indeed, but what individuals make of them depends upon what values are chosen.

If there are problems in politics and society, the idealist world view would prompt its adherents to influence value judgements, to repress unacceptable ideas (and their originators) and to intensify indoctrination. Problems are generally caused by 'all of us'; it is we who have made wrong value judgements and so acted mistakenly.

Thus it is also 'all of us' who cause problems in the environment, live unhealthily, have a wrong attitude to work and increase welfare expenditure through 'inflated expectations' or else drive up expenditure on armaments through 'exaggerated fears regarding security'.

By contrast, the realist world view pays less attention to ideas than to interests, less to individual actors on the small stage than to the large agents or macroagents in society and their relative positions of strength. Moreover, in this world view it is the macroagents which principally determine the structure and developments in society, for the sum of individual acts and of interpersonal relationships certainly does not arise outside the power positions of the macroagents in society, whether these be bureaucracies, business entrepreneurs, armies or press baronies.

It follows that from this viewpoint power is by no means confined to the state. Indeed, the power of 'the politicians' in relation to the macroagents in society tends to be seen as limited. Moreover, in the realist world view the problems of society most certainly do have something to do with the macroagents. Consequently the demand for changes is addressed not so much to the suffering microactors as to the large organizations. Problems are traced back less to subjective factors and individual decisions than to social structures and functional situations.

Furthermore, in the realist world view the material side of life plays an important part. For example, when considering the state it pays less attention to the political rhetoric of governments and parties than to the development of the state finances, less to shifts of electoral opinion than to political donations or party preferences of the media. Lastly, the realist world view believes that the idealist world view too is explained as being the expression of the opinion-forming power of the power structures in society. From this viewpoint it is above all a world picture for the public which pays up and suffers. To speak accurately, however, the macroagents too are inclined to adopt the realist world view and appraise those with whom they have dealings entirely according to the rules of a realist analysis of power and interests.

This is not the place in which to tone down the one-sidedness of this sketch by limning in the nuances. Perhaps it needs no emphasis that the realist world view too can attribute great importance to ideas, changing values or the political culture. Here we are concerned with the consequences of the two world views for analysis, and I should like to illustrate these by what I call the 'myth of instrumentality.'[7]

What is in question is the unexamined assumption that in politics and society 'actors' set themselves 'goals' which they achieve by the use of certain 'means'. On this view the agent is sovereign on two counts: he chooses both the goals and the means. According to this understanding, such 'means' include centralized bureaucracies invested with coercive powers – as 'executors' of political aims – or industries as 'instruments' in the hand of the customer or armies as executant organs of public security requirements. It is individuals, singly or jointly, who in this – obviously sovereign – fashion adopt aims and select means, as electors, consumers, politicians etc.

For example, according to this innocent world picture the elector can decide how the finances of the state are to be conducted. 'In a democratic society, the distribution of resources between the public and private sectors is roughly determined by the desires of the electorate.' (A. Downs)[8]

Describing individual decisions this way presupposes the mystification of the 'instruments', but experience does not seem to confirm the impression that the macroagents in society, with whom we are here concerned, allow themselves without further ado to be made the servants of aims that have been set for them by others.

On the contrary, ever since Hegel and Marx we have repeatedly been told about the propensity of social means to make themselves independent of the ends. This has even been seen as a present-day trend. Simmel, Gehlen and Luhmann all reject the idea that today's macro-organizations are instruments: 'Unlike the position in individual dealings . . . the ostensible objective is typically not the motive for the actions of organized systems.'[9]

In any event there is no political–sociological analysis of realism unless, following the above 'instrumentalism', we also systematically ask the question in reverse: what do the means do with the goals? What does the medical-industry complex do with the goal of 'health'? What does the military-industrial complex do with the goal of 'security'? What does the ecology industry do with the goal of 'protection of the environment'? What do the clergy do with Christendom? What does the monopoly – bureaucratic party system do with 'socialism'? The first answer to these questions must be that the 'means' use the goals as a basis for their legitimation.[10]

That is the first act of a reversal of the ends – means relationship. The second act is to specify each of the goals, which are mostly empty formulations, in terms of the real interests of their respective organizations, and here too the next question is whether and to what extent the decisions follow the arguments or the arguments follow the decisions. Is the new weapons system bought because the Defence Minister was 'worried' about the armaments of the other side or had the said weapons system perhaps been ordered years before?

Principles of analysis

My aim in what follows is not to propose an analytical concept of my own but, since we as social scientists apprehend reality through our concepts, I should like to make my viewpoint clear by reference to a number of key concepts.

My concern is with a problem-oriented political science as a realistic analysis. The main problem of politics in the developed industrial system is how to deal with (1) the organized macroagents in society, (2) their power positions, (3) their interest positions, (4) their information positions, (5) their functional positions, and (6) the potential crisis situations. ('Positions' refers to both structural and situational aspects.) The dynamic context of the whole is denoted by the concept of (7) development. Whereas this covers the objective side of the process, the concept of (8) strategy denotes the subjective side.

Let us develop the theme a little further.

(1) Large agents and macroagents in society are organized systems. They are more than and different from individual microagents (who in relation to them are often the persons affected rather than the doers). Macroagents are something other than the sum of the persons constituting them. They have indeed something akin to experiences, modes of thinking or motives, but these are not to be confused with those of people; the 'psychology' of large organizations is something different. Not even the psychology of the management explains the behavioural regularities of the macroagents in society, for the psychology of top management is often marked by conflict between the role expectations *of* the organization and personal perceptions or needs *within* the organization. A general may personally become a pacifist, but the army has other 'views'. A manager may want to escape from the competitive pressure of his firm – and unlike the firm he can do so if he wishes. A bishop may arrive at new judgements about celibacy, but the relationship of the clergy to femininity is determined by other motives; whereas people have erotic needs, organizations do not.

The reference to the 'myth of instrumentality' shows how unsatisfactory it is to describe organizations, whether industrial firms, bureaucracies, armies, churches or newspaper corporations by reference to their official aims, and it is just as misleading to explain organizations by human motives, simply because they consist of people and are managed by people. This is one of the main reasons why calls by reformers to 'think again' so often fall on deaf ears. The way individuals think must not be confused with the vested interests of corporate staffs. If reformers are to deal with organizational vested interests, they must adopt different strategies and change interest constellations.

(2) Power positions: the real subject of this enquiry was the thesis that the problem of political control has become the main problem in the industrial countries. The concept of the power position is indispensable for explaining this state of affairs.

Power positions have much to do with functional positions and vested interests. Indeed, they give added significance to the theory of power, kratology. If a branch of industry is intimately connected with the economy as a whole, as are the automobile and building industries, this creates a community of interests of formidable proportions, and the ability to mobilize this community of interests represents enormous power. If, depending on the method of calculation, from 1.7 million to 4 million employees in West Germany make their livings directly or indirectly from cars, it does not need the automobile associations to keep the production lines moving. In political terms there would be a good case for assessing the power position of a given branch of industry not only by the amount it contributes to GNP but also by the extent to which it is interwoven with the rest of the economy.

However, customer–supplier relationships are not the whole story. There are also personal relationships arising from positions on the supervisory or executive boards of groups, and above all interlocking capital. The same applies to lending or contractual relationships.

This leads to an important point: whereas in the sphere of politics power positions in coalitions are built up by dint of much effort, in business there is the *de facto* alliance by virtue of similar vested interests, which arise not only from formal linkages but also through the general solidarity of growth interests (because each contributes to and depends on growth of the macroeconomy). Therefore in matters of growth in general, business and industry really form a homogeneous power bloc.

In addition to functional interconnection there is the aspect of functional importance (which Offe calls 'functional relevance'). This is determined by which services indispensable to the social process an agent is in a position to withhold.

A further factor in power accumulation is the degree of organization. The first place to look for this is not the trade associations. Enterprises, administrations, armies etc. are already as such interest organizations. Unlike the consumers and environmental, peace and future interests, these interests are excellently organized from the start on a career basis and adequately financed. It is characteristic of the power of the macroagents in industrial societies that they nevertheless form a great number of additional interest organizations.

Power, then, is not only the result of available means of coercion and hierarchical dependence through organization and the power of command, but is also the result of functional dependencies and mobilizable interests; there is also the power to mobilize through publicity channels, propaganda and a following of sympathizers. The part played by functional and interest positions in power accumulation has long been underestimated. The impotence of the state resulting from its dependence on tax revenues from the economy and the part played by the solidarity of economic profit and growth interests in the formation of power are essential aspects of this extended analysis of power.

It also includes the effect of power formation processes. This relates to the problem of governability no less than the problems of acceptance, innovation and redistribution within developed industrial systems. This has been one of the main themes of this enquiry.

(3) Interests are fundamental and relatively stable motives for action, traceable to vital needs of individuals or functional requirements of organizations. Unlike value judgements, interests are not arbitrary but can be inferred with a high degree of plausibility because they are so strongly engrained and empirically regular. Because of this, interest-led decisions are more calculable and predictable than value judgements. This applies above all to material interest in a person's or organization's own existence and his or her immediate reproduction and posterity. Like the concept of power and other concepts central to the discourse of political science, the concept of interest is extremely important but not very precise. In most cases it can only be determined on grounds of plausibility.[11]

As so often in the sphere of politics, its negative connotation is the most precise. Many interests are not discernible until they are threatened, so the defence of interests is a specially important aspect of the matter – whether it is the defence of health, the environment, tenants or peace. It would be much more difficult to define only the interests named positively than it would be to define those named negatively. It is easier to say that noise is unbearable than to determine how much peace a person needs.

The concept of interest calls for two important qualifications, however. One of these relates to the information status. Not all infringements of interest are immediately perceptible; they have to be known about. Noise can be heard, but if the inbreathed air contains carcinogenic substances, the person affected is usually unaware of the fact – unlike the person who has caused it. Infringements of political interest often have a similar information status. Those affected by the policy know too little. Subjective deviations from objective interests are far more complicated. For example, downtrodden people tend to work off their frustration about interference they cannot fend off upon weaker people. Thus action appropriate to interests should include not only information but in the last resort sufficient capacity for conflict as well.[12] This in turn depends on power or functional positions. There is generally a good explanation for subjective deviations from objective interests. Suicide is no reason for not presuming a general interest in remaining alive.

(4) Information status is increasingly important in the developed industrial societies, especially as it is becoming more and more critical. The ever-increasing division of labour coupled with increasing interdependence in complex inter-relationships creates an enormous need for information. At the same time power positions are leading to a marked monopolization of access to information, but power positions themselves are dependent upon channels of information, as witness the marked importance of advertising and political propaganda. What makes the concept of information status so important is primarily this dependence of information flows on power positions and vested interests. This may result in information being manipulated, and it can be so self-propagating that it sometimes reflects back on the sources of the information. I maintain that the facilities for self-deception possessed by the macroagents in the bureaucracy and industry are reinforced by the macroagents' own propaganda, at least when counter-arguments can be more or less screened out. The tendency of power to lose its sense of reality is not connected only with the internal problems of processing information in the organization, but also with the information status created externally.

(5) Functional positions: functions are operational connections which are vitally necessary or at least extremely important to a social unit. Thus the concept of the functional position relates to dependencies. It has all the advantages of a functionalist approach.

This came to the fore in comparative political analysis, when it became clear how little is explained if we simply look at structures, institutions, ideologies etc. In comparisons between East and West this functionalist approach came into use in the 1960s (with 'convergence theory').[13] It was realized then that the enormous differences between the institutions, power structures, property relationships, ideologies and so on in East and West, did not provide an explanation of the striking 'functional' similarities between the systems, from social policy to research policy. The marxist analysis of society was in any event always a functionalist analysis in that it always looked at the 'function' of subsystems in the development of the overall nexus of relationships.

Following Parsons, authors such as Almond, Verba, Pye and others developed a functionalist approach to political science,[14] which from our present perspective is useful in that it too makes the dynamics of the development of overall relationships accessible. After that the story begins not with the description of the structures (of programmes, institutions, forms of authority or elites and their history), but with the functional connection of the system in the superordinate context and its development. In the first step, only the 'input' into the system from outside and its reactions as an 'output' are of interest. Who is acting within the system, on the basis of which ideologies and past experiences, is of secondary importance for the moment. What primarily counts is the output or outcome, e.g. the movement of state expenditures. What takes place within the system is treated as a 'black box'. If the output does not furnish a sufficient explanation recourse is had to the inner workings – and in such cases this may be of great importance.

The further advantage of functionalism, whether of the bourgeois or marxist variety, resides in the fact that it investigates the role of the state in the process of social development instead of contenting itself with a static description of political forms. Finally it has the advantage of being problem-oriented; the political system is viewed from the aspect of responding to challenges. This is important for a political science that is practice-related.

(6) Problem-oriented functional observation necessarily leads to an increased interest in crisis situations.[15] This is not due to a negativist philosophy, but to the fact that from a functionalist viewpoint crisis situations are fundamental and ambivalent stages of development. They create a heightened pressure for change, which may lead either to innovative advance of the system or else to severe losses and a regression to earlier stages of development. Thus with careful observation crisis analysis can become a heuristic principle or means of comprehension. Methodologically, crisis management is regarded as the ultimately decisive functional problem of the system.

In this process crisis has on the one hand an objective side as a functional phase tending to malfunction. For example, there is objectively a critical situation if the state regularly spends more than it receives, or if mass unemployment continues to increase. But on the other hand this situation must be subjectively perceived and transposed to make it a political issue. Consequently the political crisis that has become public is characterized by malfunctions that are viewed by specific affected parties as a threat which must be averted with all the means at their disposal. Typically this gives rise to a dual embarrassment, first of those immediately affected and then of governments, if governments are effectively confronted with the crisis situation in society.

At the heart of this definition of crisis, however, are the available means. In situations of social impotence it is often politically virtually impracticable even to admit the existence of crises. Crises are then suppressed at pre-political levels; suppressed youth unemployment for example is then expressed as rioting, criminality or alcoholism. Conversely the means may be so abundant that even minor hiccups can be termed crises and may touch off excessive reactions. The military action taken by the United States against Libya in April 1986 was a symptom of power positions which permitted the luxury of exaggerated perceptions of crisis. By contrast, in the areas of malfunction in domestic politics dealt with in this book, governments both in East and West have a strong propensity to delay crises. This also characterizes (weak) power positions. In such cases, pressure for change of critical proportions does not lead to a higher level of development.

(7) This is the decisive correlation: crises potentially lead to development. If we consider the history of the last 200 years, large waves, or rather stages, of development through crisis in the industrial countries can be discerned.[16] By development I mean the institutionalization of a new pattern of crisis management. In this process crisis management is more than just displacing problems of the system into the dim corners of society that are unlikely to offer resistance. Development always has something to do with innovation, and one of the central concerns of this book has been with the productivity of the crisis mechanism, for it can be weakened in the long term so that crisis is less and less the precursor of development.

Development is something different from the 'trend'. It is of course always extremely important to perceive the trend. Well-grounded social science will always be striving to produce predictive analyses which take account of the dynamic laws of a social entity, endeavouring to determine which way it is going and to appraise the consequences for those affected by it. In times of social change, when, for example, conditions on the world market are undergoing fundamental change, this will frequently eventuate in forecasts of crises on the lines of 'crisis if the current trend is maintained'. The makers of these prophecies want them to be falsified – by deliberate counter-measures and by development. Our problem today is that too many crisis forecasts of this kind are *not* falsified.

(8) This leads on to the concept of strategy, which means above all systematic decisions against the trend. The trend consists of the way situations develop under their own momentum, and is primarily determined by the overall structure of functional, interest and power positions. 'Trend' means the long-term process of everyday movements. Strategy means consciously changing their direction, with subordinate tactical steps.

I consider the concept of strategy to be important, in order to avoid the mistaken impression that history is nothing but an inevitable process determined by power positions and vested interests. Nor is it necessarily the history of the macroagents in society, for there are counter-strategies to their strategies, and in crisis situations these can often be extremely successful.

Notes

Chapter 1 Introduction and Overview

1   On the theory of long-term economic cycles, see J. Huber: 'Modell und Theorie der langen Wellen', in M. Jänicke (ed.) *Vor uns die goldenen neunziger Jahre? Langzeitprognosen auf dem Prüfstand*, Munich 1985.

2   A. Wagner: *Grundlegung der politischen Ökonomie, Teil I: Grundlagen der Volkswirtschaft*, 3rd edn., Leipzig 1983, p. 892 Cf. J. Kohl: *Staatsausgaben in Westeuropa. Analysen zur langfristigen Entwicklung der öffentlichen Finanzen*, Frankfurt am Main and New York 1984.

3   M.J. Crozier, S.P. Huntington and J. Watanuki: *The Crisis of Democracy*, New York 1975 (A Trilateral Commission study). R. Rose (ed.): *Challenge to Governance: Studies in Overloaded Polities*, Beverly Hills 1980. W. Hennis, P. Graf Kielmansegg, and U. Matz (eds): *Regierbarkeit. Studien zu ihrer Problematisierung*, 2 vols, Stuttgart 1977 and 1979. C. Offe: 'Ungovernability: on the renaissance of conservative theories of crisis', in J. Habermas (ed.) *Observations on 'The Spiritual Situation of the Age'*, Cambridge, Mass., 1984. K. von Beyme: 'Unregierbarkeit in westlichen Demokratien', *Leviathan* No. 1, 1984, pp. 39ff.

4   C. Schmitt: *Der Hüter der Verfassung*. Tübingen 1931. Vgl. M. Jänicke: *Totalitäre Herrschaft. Anatomie eines politischen Begriffs*, Berlin 1971, pp. 36ff.

5   M. Jänicke: *Wie das Industriesystem von seinen Mißständen profitiert*, Opladen 1979. M. Jänicke: 'Zur Theorie des Staatsversagens', in P. Grottian (ed.) 'Folgen reduzierten Wachstums für Politikfelder', *Politische Vierteljahresschrift, Special issue*, no. 11, 1980. M. Jänicke: 'Versorgung und Entsorgung im superindustriellen System', in J. Matthes (ed.) *Lebenswelt und soziale Probleme. Verhandlungen des 20. Deutschen Soziologentages zu Bremen 1980*. Frankfurt am Main and New York 1981. M. Jänicke: 'Superindustrialismus und Postindustrialismus – Langzeitperspektiven von Umweltbelastung und Umweltschutz,' in M. Jänicke, U.E. Simonis and G. Weigmann (eds) *Wissen für die Umwelt*, Berlin 1985.

6   L. Späth: *Wende in die Zukunft*, Reinbeck 1985; K.H. Biedenkopf: *Die neue Sicht der Dinge*, Munich 1985. O. Lafontaine: *Der andere Fortschritt*, Hamburg 1985. W. Roth: *Der Weg aus der Krise*, Munich 1985.

Chapter 2 The Role of the State in the Industrial System

1   The following section partly follows relevant passages in my book *Wie das Industriesystem von seinen Mißständen profitiert*, Opladen 1979, pp. 20 ff.

2   See chapter 1.

3   Cf. R. Aron: *18 Lectures on Industrial Society*, London 1967. J.K. Galbraith: *The New Industrial State*, London 1972.

4   Cf. J. O'Connor: *The Fiscal Crisis of the State*, London and New York 1973. R.R. Grauhan and R. Hickel (eds.): Krise des Steuerstaats?' *Leviathan, Special issue* No. 1, 1978 (introduction). E. Altvater: 'Zu einigen Problemen des "Krisenmanagement" in der kapitalistischen Gesellschaft', in M. Jänicke (ed.) *Herrschaft und Krise*, Opladen 1973, pp. 170ff.

5   M. Weber: *Basic Concepts in Sociology*, London 1962.

6   M. Jänicke: *Wie das Industriesystem*, pp. 23ff.

7   *Wirtschaft und Statistik* no. 7, 1984, p. 586.

8   M. Jänicke: *Wie das Industriesystem* pp. 26ff.

9   Ibid., pp. 28ff.

10   Ibid., pp. 33ff.

11   G. Winter: *Das Vollzugsdefizit im Wasserrecht*, Berlin 1975, p. 60.

12   R. Hilferding: *Das Finanzkapital*, Frankfurt am Main 1968 (originally published 1910). Cf. H. Arndt: *Wirtschaftliche Macht*, Munich 1980, pp. 13ff.

13   H. Marcuse: *The One-Dimensional Man*, Boston 1964 (originally published 1964).

14   T. Eschenburg: *Herrschaft der Verbände?* Stuttgart 1955. Cf. R.G. Heinze: *Verbändepolitik und "Neokorporatismus"*, Opladen 1981. A. Cawson (ed): *Organized Interests and the State*, London 1985.

15   M. Olson: *The Logic of Collective Action*, Cambridge 1965. C. Offe: 'Politische Herrschaft und Klassenstrukturen', in C. Kress and D. Senghaas (eds) *Politikwissenschaft. Eine Einführung in ihre Probleme*, Frankfurt am Main 1969.

16   C. Offe: 'Crisis of crisis management: elements of a political crisis theory', *International Journal of Politics*, 6, no. 3, 1976, pp. 28–67. Cf. M. Jänicke: 'Was heißt Alternativpolitik in unserer Gesellschaft?' In Landeszentrale f. polit. Bildung des Landes Nordrhein-Westfalen (ed.): *Ziele für die Zukunft-Enstscheidungen für Morgen*, Cologne 1982.

17   SIPRI (ed.): *World Armament and Disarmament. Yearbook 1984*, London 1984. S. Behrend: 'Militärausgaben. Ein internationaler Vergleich von Militärausgaben in 18 ausgewählten OECD-Ländern', unpublished manuscript, Free University of Berlin, Department of Political Science, 1985.

18   This complaint goes back to Laski. J. Agnoli and P. Brückner: *Die Transformation der Demokratie*, Frankfurt am Main 1968, p. 57 *et passim*. Cf. as a literature survey K. Kluxen (ed.): *Parlamentarismus*. Cologne and Berlin 1967.

19   Cf. C.C. Schweitzer: *Der Abgeordnete im parlamentarischen Regierungssystem der Bundesrepublik*, Opladen 1979.

20   N. Poultantzas: *Staatstheorie*, Hamburg 1978, p. 211.

21   N. Luhmann: *Legitimation durch Verfahren*, Neuwied and Berlin 1969, pp. 157ff.

22 Carl Schmitt used this expression as early as 1931 with a quite different political connotation (in support of the conservative–authoritarian argument of ungovernability), M. Jänicke: *Totalitäre Hervschaft*, Berlin 1971, p. 37.

23 N. Luhmann: *Macht*, Stuttgart 1975, pp. 107ff.

24 Cf. C. Böhret et al.: *Innenpolitik und politische Theorie*, Opladen 1979, pp. 282ff.

25 Ch. E. Lindblom: 'Inkrementalismus: die Lehre vom "Sich-Durchwursteln" ' (originally published 1959), Reprinted in W.-D. Narr and C. Offe (eds): *Wohlfahrtsstaat und Massenloyalität*, Cologne 1975.

26 K. Zimmermann and F.G. Müller: *Umweltschutz als neue politische Aufgabe*, Frankfurt am Main and New York 1985, pp. 285ff.

27 Calculated from *Statistisches Jahrbuch für die Bundesrepublik Deutschland 1985*, Stuttgart and Mainz 1985, pp. 439, 91.

28 Ibid., pp. 92, 439.

29 Ibid., p. 439.

Chapter 3 The Theory of State Failure

1 R.A. Musgrave, P.B. Musgrave and L. Kullmer: Die öffentlichen Finanzen in Theorie und Praxis, vol. 1, Tübingen 1978 (Originally published 1973), pp. 5ff.

2 H.C. Recktenwald: 'Unwirtschaftlichkeit im Staatssektor. Elemente einer Theorie des ökonomischen "Staatsversagens" ', in *Hambuger Jahrbuch für Wirtschafts-und Gesellschaftspolitik*, Tübingen 1978, pp. 155–66. Also *Markt und Staat. Fundamente einer freiheitlichen Ordnung in Wirtschaft und Politik*, Göttingen 1980. And A. Rosenschon: *Verschwendung in Markt und Staat*, Diss. Göttingen 1980. St Ruß-Mohl: 'Kann der Markt, was der Staat nicht kann? Anmerkungen zur ökonomischen Theorie des Staatsversagens', supplement to weekly, *Das Parlament* 5 April 1980. P. Koslowski: 'Markt-und Demokratieversagen?', *Politische Vierteljahresschrift*, 24, No. 2, 1983. L. Thürmer: Bürokratie und Effizienz staatlichen Handelns, Berlin and Munich 1984. H. Hanusch (ed.): *Anatomy of Government Deficiencies*, Berlin and Heidelberg 1983.

3 M. Jänicke: 'Zur Theorie des Staatsversagens', supplement to weekly *Das Parlament* of 5 April 1980. M. Jänicke: *Wie das Insdustriesystem von seinen Mißständen profitiert*, Opladen 1979.

4 Cf. Ch. E. Lindblom: *Jenseits von Markt und Staat. Eine Kritik der politischen und ökonomischen Systeme*, Stuttgart 1980 (originally published in 1977) pp. 141ff.

5 R.A. Musgrave, P.B. Musgrave and L. Kullmer: *Die öffentlichen Finanzen in Theorie und Praxis*, vol. 1, Tübingen 1978, p. 8.

6 J. O'Connor: *Die Finanzkrise des Staates*, Frankfurt am Main 1974, pp. 74ff.

7 M. Jänicke: 'Versorgung und Entsorgung im superindustriellen System', in J. Matthes (Ed.): *Lebenswelt und soziale Probleme. Verhandlungen des 20. Deutschen Soziologentages zu Bremen 1980*, Frankfurt am Main and New York 1981.

8 *Statistisches Jahrbuch für die Bundesrepublik Deutschland*, current annual sets.

9 M. Jänicke: *Wie das Industriesystem* pp. 88ff.

10   Ibid., pp. 104ff.
11   Ibid., p. 9.

Chapter 4 Public Health and Protection of the Environment

1   'Health Spending: Its Growth and Control', *OECD Observer* no. 137, November 1985.
2   *Satistical Abstracts of the United States 1985*, Washington, D.C., 1984, p. 96.
3   'Ausgaben für Gesundhheit 1985', *Wirtschaft und Statistik* no. 8, 1987, p. 655.
4   'Gesundheitskosten: Augen zu', *Der Spiegel* no. 48, 1985, pp. 30 ff. Cf. *Gutachten 1985/86 des SVR*, Bundestagsdrucksache 10/4295, pp. 166ff.
5   *Wirtshaft und Statistik* no. 4, 1984 and no. 12 (1980).
6   *Wirtschaft und Statistik* no. 1, 1984.
7   *DDR Handbuch*, vol. 2, Cologne 1985, p. 1369.
8   M. Jänicke: 'Luftverschmutzung: Staub gleichmäßig verteilt', *Natur* No. 6, June 1981, pp. 94ff.
9   Vgl. H. Schäfer (ed.): *Folgen der Zivilisation*, Frankfurt am Main 1974. H.-H. Abholz et al. (eds): *Risikofaktorenmedizin*, Berlin and New York 1982. World Health Organization (WHO): *Global Strategy for Health for All by the year 2000*, Geneva (WHO) 1979. G. Göckenjan: *Kurieren und Staat machen*, Frankurt and Main 1985.
10   *Wirtschaft und Statistik* no. 9, 1986, p. 748.
11   H. Schäfer: 'Hinweise auf Umweltschäden aus Lebenserwartung, spezifischen Sterblichkeiten, Sterbeziffern und Krankheitshäufigkeiten', in H. Schäfer, *Folgen der Zivilisation*, pp. 72ff.
12   P. Saunders and F. Klau: *The Role of the Public Sector*, Paris (OECD) 1985, p. 134. The authors also give the following data on the numbers of working days lost through employee sickness (p. 152):

	1960	1970	1981
France	13.2	13.3	13.6
Ireland	19.5	25.6	33.8
Italy	–	12.7	17.2
Luxembourg	11.2	11.0	12.1
Netherlands	5.3	7.7	8.5
Sweden	13.2	19.9	22.8
United Kingdom	13.8	16.7	20.0

13   Saunders and Klau, *Role of Public Sector*, p. 135.
14   Ibid., pp. 132, 134
15   *Statistisches Jahrbuch 1989 für die Bundesrepublik Deutschland*, Stuttgart 1989, p. 586.

16   Ibid.
17   *Statistical Abstracts of the United States,* Washington, D.C., current annual sets.
18   'Investitionsboom beim Umweltschutz', *Umwelt* (BMI) no. 2, 1986, pp. 1ff.
      'Umweltpolitik sichert Arbeitsplätze', *Umwelt* (BMI) no. 5, 1985, p. 4. 'Arbeit
      und Umweltschutz (1)', *Wirtschaftswoche* 12 April 1985, pp. 97ff.
19   OECD: *The State of the Environment 1985,* Paris 1985, p. 242.
20   Ibid., p. 145 *OECD Environmental Data. Compendium 1987,* Paris (OECD)
      1987, pp. 124ff.
21   Environmental data for the RFG, Umweltbundesamt: *Daten zur Umwelt 1988/89,*
      Berlin 1989. E.R. Koch: *Die Lage der Nation 1985/86 - Umweltatlas der Bundes-
      republik,* Hamburg 1985.
22   OECD: *The State of the Environment,* p. 53.
23   'The state of the environment in the OECD countries', *OECD Observer* no. 135,
      July 1985, p. 19 Cf. *Umwelt* (BMI) no. 4, 1984, p. 4.
24   Ibid., p. 25.
25   G. Zellentin: 'Militarisierung und Umweltzerstörung in der Bundesrepublik', in
      M. Jänicke, U.E. Simonis and G. Weigmann (eds) *Wissen für die Umwelt,* Berlin
      1985, pp. 155ff.
26   K.-H. Hübler: 'Die Zerstörung des Umweltmediums Boden', in Jänicke, Simonis
      and Weigmann, *Wissen für die Umwelt,* pp. 95ff.
27   OECD: *The State of the Environment,* pp. 163ff.
28   *Umwelt* (BMI) No. 5, 1988, p. 212. Cf. 'Potemkinsche Anlagen', *Der Spiegel*
      no. 37, (1984), pp. 56ff.
29   M. Jänicke: *'Internationaler Umweltschutz. Versuch einer Leistungsbilanz',* Umwelt
      (published by VDI) no. 4, 1976, pp. 315ff. Cf. M. Jänicke: 'Blauer Himmel über
      den Industriestädten - eine optische Täuschung', in M. Jänicke (ed.) *Umwelt-
      politik.,* Opladen 1978.
30   Statistisches Bundesamt, *Umweltinformationen der Statistik,* Stuttgart und
      Mainz 1988, p. 122.
31   R.-D. Brunowsky and L. Wicke: *Der Öko-Plan. Durch Umweltschutz zum neuen
      Wirtschaftswunder,* Munich 1984, p. 36.
32   L. Wicke: *Die Ökologischen Milliarden,* Munich 1986, pp. 123ff.
33   *Environmental Quality. The Ninth Annual Report of the Council on Environmental
      Quality,* Washington, D.C., 1978, p. 420.
34   'The Greek environment', *OECD Observer* no. 125, November 1983, p. 29.
35   'Umweltschäden überfordern Assekuranz', *Süddeutsche Zeitung* 29 April 1985.
36   H.-J. Ewers (Project leader): *Methodische Probleme der monetären Bewertung eines
      komplexen Umweltschadens am Beispiel des Waldsterbens in der Bundesrepublik
      Deutschland,* Technische Universität Berlin 1985, p. 6 *et passim.*
37   M. Jänicke: *Umweltpolitische Prävention als ökologische Modernisierung und
      Strukturpolitik,* Wissenschaftszentrum Berlin 1984 (IIUG dp 84-1). Also
      'Beschäftigungspolitik', *Natur* no. 4 1983, pp. 58ff (part of the journal's 'alterna-
      tive government declaration'). For the stages of strategic environmental policy
      see J. Gerau: 'Zur polit. Ökologie d. Industrialisierung des Umweltschutzes', in
      M. Jänicke (ed.) *Umweltpolitik.*

38 R.-U. Sprenger et al. *Struktur und Entwicklung der Umweltschutzindustrie in der Bundesrepublik Deutschland,* Berlin 1983, p. 21.   .

39 Environment Agency, Japan: *Quality of the Environment in Japan 1976,* Tokyo, undated pp. 24f.

40 Ch. Maas and H.-J. Ewers: *Wirkungen umweltpolitischer Maßnahmen auf das Innovationsverhalten von Galvanikbetrieben,* Wissenschaftszentrum Berlin 1983 (IIUG dp 83-12). R.F. Nolte: 'Innovation und Umweltschutz', in A.A., Ullmann and K. Zimmermann (eds) *Umweltpolitik im Wandel,* Frankfurt am Main and New York 1982.

41 M. Jänicke: 'Arbeitsplätze durch umweltgerchtes Wirtschaften', in J. Berger, J. Müller and R. Pfriem (eds) 'Kongreß Zunkunft der Arbeit', Bielefeld 1982', pp. 296ff. V. Hauff: 'Für eine ökologische Modernisierung der Volkswirtschaft', in V. Hauff and M. Müller (eds) *Umweltpolitik am Scheideweg,* Munich 1985.

Chapter 5 Transport and Energy Policy

1   Bundesministerium des Innern (Federal Ministry of the Interior): Was Sie schon immer über Auto und Umwelt wissen wollten, Stuttgart and Mainz 1983, p. 9 Cf. M. Burkhart: *Die gesellschaftl. Kosten des Autoverkehrs,* Freiburg 1980.

2   *Was Sie schon immer* ibid., pp. 8ff.

3   Umweltbundesamt: *Daten für die Umwelt,* Berlin 1984, p. 160.

4   *Environmental Quality 1981. 12th Annual Report of the Council on Environmental Quality,* Washington, D.C., undated, p. 246.

5   'From innovation to creation, Japan charts a new course', *Time* 11 March 1985.

6   K. Traube: 'Massenmotorisierung: Probleme und Auswege', in M. Jänicke, U.E. Simonis and G. Weigmann (eds) *Wissen für die Umwelt,* Berlin 1985, p. 131.

7   H. Holzapfel, K. Traube and O. Ullrich: *Autoverkehr 2000,* Karlsruhe 1985, p. 114.

8   'Ein paar Zahlen reichten', *Der Spiegel* no. 48, 1985, pp. 19ff.

9   Holzapfel et al., *Autoverkehr 2000,* p. 63f.

10 *Woche im Bundestag,* 5 February 1986, p. 30.

11 'Energieverbrauch des Verkehrs in der Bundesrepublik Deutschland', *DIW-Wochenbericht* 3/86, 16 January 1986, p. 30.

12 A. Löw: 'Stagnierender Energiebedarf auch bei wachsender Wirtschaft', *Zeitschrift für Energiewirtschaft* no. 2, 1985, p. 9.

13 M. Jänicke: 'Zukunftsforschung: Erstens kommt es anders und zweitens als man wünscht', *Natur* no. 7, 1984, pp. 39ff. K. Traube and O. Ullrich: *Billiger Atomstrom? Wie die Interessen der Elektrizitätswirtschaft die Energiepolitik bestimmen,* Reinbek 1982, pp. 16, 168.

14 K. Traube: *Plutoniumwirtschaft? Das Finanzdebakel von Brutreaktor und Wiederaufbereitung,* Reinbek 1984. K.M. Meyer-Abich and R. Ueberhorst (eds): *AUSgebrütet - Argumente zur Brutreaktorpolitik,* Basel, Boston and Stuttgart 1985. O. Keck: *Der schnelle Brüter. Eine Fallstudie über Entscheidungsprozesse in der Großtechnik,* Frankfurt am Main and New York 1984.

15 'RWE: Eine Mischung aus Allmacht und Filz', *Der Spiegel* no. 9, 1986, p. 84.

16 Ibid. 'RWE: Gestörte Kontakte', *Wirtschaftswoche* 28 June 1985. AG Atomindustrie and AG Chem. Industrie (eds): *RWE – Ein Riese mit Ausstrahlung*, Cologne 1984. See also G. Karweina: *Der Strom-Staat, Hamburg 1984. St. Kohler: Geschichte der deutschen Elektrizitätswirtschaft und ihre Auswirkungen auf die kommunale und regionale Energieversorgung*, Freiburg 1984. J. Radkau: *Aufstieg und Krise der deutschen Atomwirtschaft*, Reinbek 1983. K.M. Meyer- Abich and B. Schefold: *Die Grenzen der Atomwirtschaft*, Munich 1986. K. Traube et al.: *Nach dem Super-GAU. Die Konsequenzen aus Tschernobyl*, Reinbek 1986.

17 *Concession agreement. Addendum K* to BEWAG Statute, 1977 edn.

18 *BEWAG Business reports.*

19 *RWE Business reports.*

20 Senate's answer to interpellation by the Alternative List group. *Abgeordetenhaus v. Berlin, 9. Wahlperiode, Drucksache* 9/630, p. 2.

21 *Süddeutsche Zeitung* 7 February 1986.

22 Preisamt: *Vermerk, Betr: Strom-Tarifpreise der BEWAG*, 11 December 1979.

23 Der Präsident des Abgeordnetenhauses von Berlin. Stenogr. Dienst: *Wortprotokoll der Enquete-Kommission 'Zukünftige Energiepolitik'*. 14. Sitzung, 10 June 1983.

24 Ibid.

25 W. Mönig et al.: *Konzentration und Wettberwerb in der Energiewirtschaft*, Munich 1977. G. Bruche: *Elektrizitätsversorgung und Staatsfunktion*, Frankurt am Main 1977. F.-J. Holker and F. Raudszus: *Die Konzentration der Energiewirtschaft*, Frankfurt am Main and New York 1985.

26 P. Hennicke et al.: *Die Energie-Wende ist möglich. Die neue Energiepolitik der Kommunen*, Frankfurt am Main 1985.

27 Ch. Flavin: 'The growth of small-scale power', *Economic Impact* no. 3 1985, pp. 47ff.

28 H. Kitschelt: Politik und Energie. Frankfurt am Main and New York 1983, p. 378.

29 J. Goldemberg et al.: *Energy for a Sustainable World*, New Delhi 1988.

Chapter 6 Structural Economic Policy

1 W. Fucks: *Formeln zur Macht. Prognosen über Völker*, Wirtschaft, Potentiale, Reinbek 1967 (first published 1965).

2 R.B. Reich: *The Next American Frontier*, New York 1983. R.B. Reich: *An Industrial Policy for America*, Washington, D.C., 1983. Cf. *OECD Positive Adjustment Policies*, Paris 1983. E.E. Driscoll and J.H. Behrman (eds): *National Industrial Policies*, Cambridge, Mass., 1984.

3 W. Hauff and F.W. Scharpf: *Modernisierung der Volkswirtschaft. Technologiepolitik als Structurpolitik*, Frankfurt am Main and Cologne 1975, Cf. F.W. Scharpf: *Politischer Immobilismus und ökonom. Krise*, Kronberg 1977.

4 Hauff and Scharpf, *Modernisierung*, pp. 117, 113.

5 *Wirtschaftlicher und sozialer Wandel in der Bundesrepublik Deutschland. Gutachten*

der Kommission, published by BM für Arbeit u. Sozialordnung, Göttingen 1977, pp. 227ff, also pp. 77ff, 119ff.

6   G. Mensch: *Das Technologische Patt. Innovationen überwinden die Depression*, Frankfurt am Main 1975, p. 21.

7   M. Jänicke, H. Mönch and Th. Ranneberg: *Umweltentlastung durch Struktur-wandel*, Wissenschaftszentrum Berlin 1986 (IIUG dp 86–1).

8   Japan Institute of International Affairs: *White Papers of Japan 1980–1981*, Tokyo 1981.

9   Jänicke, Mönch and Ranneberg, *Umweltentlastung* pp. 19ff., 28.

10 G. Kirsch: *Strukturpolitik - Ursache oder Therapie gesellschaftlicher Sklerose?* Wissenschaftszentrum Berlin 1985 (IIM/IP 85–7), Summary.

11 'Spritzen vom Staat', *Wirtschaftswoche* 27 November 1981, p. 17. Cf. 'Markt-macht Staat: Verhöhnt und verhätschelt', *Wirtschaftswoche* 13 January 1984.

12 Quote from B. Gahlen: *Strukturerhaltung als Behinderung der internationalen Wettbewersfähigkeit der deutschen Wirtschaft*, Wissenschaftszentrum Berlin 1985 (IIM/IP 85–8), p. 12.

13 R.I. Kirland, Jr: 'Are service jobs good jobs?' *Economic Impact* No. 4, 1985, p. 18.

14 F. Springmann: *Der Einfluss der bestehenden Besteuerung von Ressourcen und Arbeit auf ihren Einsatz in der Bundesrepublik Deutschland*, Technische Universität Berlin, Department 18, 1986. Cf. H.C. Binswanger et al: *Arbeit ohne Umweltzerstörung*, Frankfurt am Main 1983. H.G. Nutzinger, A. Zahrut (eds): Öko-Steuern, Karlsruhe 1989. OECD: Economic Instruments for Environmental Protection, Paris 1989.

Chapter 7 State Failure as State Indebtedness

1   'Trotz Steuerentlastung weiterer Rückgang der Staatsdefizite', *DIW-Wochenbericht* no. 50/85, 12 December 1985, p. 565. Cf. *Wirtschaftswoche* 14 September 1984, p. 18, and 15 July 1988.

2   'Öffentliche Schulden 1984', *Wirtschaft und Statistik* no. 6, 1986, p. 488.

3   P. Saunders and F. Klau: *The Role of the Public Sector. Causes and Consequences of the Growth of Government*, Paris (OECD) 1985, pp. 29, 32ff, 36.

4   'Interview with the Belgian Prime Minister Martens', *Der Spiegel* 7 October 1985. 'Ländertest Belgien', *Wirtschaftswoche* 10 August 1984.

5   Cf. *OECD Observer* 152, June–July 1988, p. 34.

6   A. Pfeiffer: 'Die Strategie der Gemeinschaft zum Abbau der Arbeitlosigkeit', *EG-Magazin* No. 1, 1986, p. 8.

7   'Finanzplanung von Bund und Ländern 1985–1989', *Wirtschaft und Statistik* no. 1. 1986, p. 63.

8   K.-P. Schmid: 'Früchte des Sparens'. *Die Zeit* 27 December 1985, p. 25.

9   Cf. 'Öffentliche Schulden 1987', *Wirtschaft und Statistik* no. 6, 1988, p. 437.

10 Ibid., p. 438.

11 'Bloated with heavy debt', *Time* 15 July 1985. Cf. 'That monster deficit', *Time* 5 March 1984. 'Reagan erwartet 4 Prozent Wachstum', *Süddeutsche Zeitung* 9 February 1986.

12 'Bloated with heavy debt'.
13 Calculated after Saunders and Klau, *Role of Public Sector*, pp. 51ff.
14 Ibid., p. 81.
15 *Statistical Abstracts of the United States 1986*, Washington, D.C., 1985, p. 310 Saunders and Klau, *Role of Public Sector*, pp. 80ff.
16 *Statistisches Jahrbuch für die Bundesrepublik Deutschland, Ausgabe 1972 und 1985*, Stuttgart and Mainz 1972 and 1985.
17 According to annual reports of BEWAG and RWE. See above, chapter 5.
18 *Die Zeit*, 24 August 1988.
19 'Öffentliche Finanzen 1985', *Wirtschaft und Statistik* no. 4, 1986, p. 313.
20 *Statistical Abstracts of the United States 1985*, Washington, D.C., p. 314. 'A hard look at the fine print', *Time* 10 June 1985, p. 33.
21 'Unternehmen: Schwerer Schaden', *Der Spiegel* no. 38, 1985, p. 178
22 'Subventionspolitik – Bestandsaufnahme und Bewertung. Zur Entwicklung der Subventionen seit 1970', *DIW-Wochenbericht* 20/84, 17 May 1984. Cf. Deutsches Institut für Wirtschaftsforschung: *Erhöhter Handlungsbedarf im Strukturwandel*, Berlin (DIW) 1983, pp. 55ff. E. Gerken, K.H. Jüttemeier, K.-W. Schatz and K.-D. Schmidt: *Subventionsabbau in der Bundesrepublik Deutschland*, Institut für Weltwirtschaft an der Universität Kiel, October 1985. 'Subventionen', *Wirtschaftswoche* 11 October 1985 and 18 October 1985.
23 'Subventionspolitik', p. 236 (own summary).
24 Ibid., p. 237.
25 G. Bruche and B. Reissert: *Die Finanzierung der Arbeitsmarktpolitik-System, Effektivität, Reformansätze*, Frankfurt am Main and New York 1985.
26 M. Kück: 'Alternative Ökonomie in der Bundesrepublik', Supplement to weekly *Das Parlament* 10 August 1985, p. 31
27 'Öffentliche Schulden 1987', p. 437
28 *Statistical Abstracts of the United States 1985*, p. 261
29 Ministry of Finance: *The 1984 Medium Term Survey of the Swedish Economy*, Stockholm 1984, pp. 186ff.
30 'The U.S. Economy: 1978–1980', *Economic Impact* no. 2, 1979. Cf. *OECD Observer* No. 138, January 1986, p. 28.
31 Ministry of Finance: *The Swedish Economy 1971–1975 and the General Outlook up to 1990*, Stockholm 1971, p. 314.
32 Ministry of Finance, *1984 Medium Term Survey*, p. 445.
33 'A beastly question', *Time* 15 October 1984, p. 49.
34 Cf. 'Reagan erwartet 4 Prozent Wachstum'.
35 Quoted from M. Jänicke (ed.): *Vor uns die goldenen neunziger Jahre? Langzeitprognosen auf dem Prüfstand*, Munich 1985, p. 174.
36 D.R. Cameron: 'The expansion of the public economy: a comparative analysis', *American Political Science Review* 72, no. 4, 1978, pp. 1243ff. Cf. M.G. Schmidt: 'The growth of the tax state' in Ch.L. Taylor (ed.), *Why Governments Grow. Measuring Public Sector Size*, Beverly Hills, London and New Delhi 1983.
37 Saunders and Klau, *Role of Public Sector*, pp. 29, 73. 'The OECD Member Countries', *OECD Observer* no. 139, March 1986.

38 Cf. G. Junne: 'Der strukturpolitische Wettlauf zwischen den kapitalistischen Industrieländern', *Politische Vierteljahresschrift* p. 25, no. 2, 1984, pp. 134ff.

Chapter 8 Superindustrialism and Post-industrialism

1   D. Bell, *The Reforming of General Education*, New York 1966, pp. 301ff. In 1967 Herman Kahn and Anthony Wiener defined the post-industrial society by characteristics such as the predominance of service industries, the innovative role of the state, the welfare state, pervasive direction of society, the 'learning society' and a decline in work-, achievement- and promotion-oriented attitudes. H. Kahn and A.J. Wiener: *The Year 2000*, New York 1967.

2   D. Bell: *The Coming of Post-Industrial Society*, New York 1973. The theory originated with Colin Clark: *The Conditions of Economic Progress*, London and New York 1940. See also A.G.B. Fisher: 'Production – primary, secondary and tertiary', *Economic Record* 15, 1939, pp. 24ff. J. Fourastié: *Die grosse Hoffnung des zwanzigsten Jahrhunderts*, Cologne 1954. L. Kern (ed.): *Probleme der post-industriellen Gesellschaft*, Cologne 1976. J.I. Gershuny and I. Miles: *The New Service Economy*, London 1983. C. Offe: *Arbeitsgesellschaft: Strukturprobleme und Zukunftsaussichten*, Frankfurt am Main and New York 1984, pp. 229ff.

3   H. Kahn: *Die Zukunft der Welt (1980-2000)*, Vienna 1980 (originally published 1979), p. 267.

4   Drawing on my paper 'Superindustrialismus und Postindustrialismus – Langzeitperspektiven von Umweltbelastung und Umweltschutz', in M. Jänicke, U.E. Simonis and Weigmann (eds) *Wissen für die Umwelt*, Berlin 1985, pp. 237ff.

5   G. Wersig (ed.): *Informatisierung und Gesellschaft*, Munich 1983. H.I. Schiller: *Die Verteilung des Wissens. Informationen im Zeitalter der grossen Konzerne*, Frankfurt am Main and New York 1984. A. Von Schoeler (ed.): Informationsgesellschaft oder Überwachungsstaat? Opladen 1985. P. Otto and Ph. Sonntag: *Wege in die Informationsgesellschaft*, Munich 1985. M. Jänicke: 'Superindustrialismus und Postindustrialismus', p. 257. B. Mettler-Maibohm: *Prolegomena einer Medienökologie*, Wissenschaftszentrum Berlin 1985 (IIUG dp 85–22). 'Informatics – is there a choice?', *Development* no. 1, 1985.

6   E. Mandel: *Der Spätkapitalismus*, Frankfurt am Main 1972. C. Offe: *Strukturprobleme des kapitalistischen Staates*, Frankfurt am Main 1972. J. Habermas: *Legitimationsprobleme im Spätkapitalismus*, Frankfurt am Main 1973. E. Altvater et al.: *Rahmenbedingungen und Schranken staatlichen Handelns*, Frankfurt am Main 1976.

7   H.H. Angermüller and H. Kolbe (eds): *Monopolmacht in der Krise. Zur politischen Labilität des staatsmonopolistische Kapitalismus*, East Berlin 1985.

8   J. O'Connor: *Die Finanzkrise des Staates*, Frankfurt am Main 1974 (1973), pp. 68ff., 252ff.

9   'Welthandel: Empfindlich gestört', *Wirtschaftswoche* 22 June 1984. G.

Feketekuty and K. Hauser: 'Information technology and trade services', *Economic Impact* No. 4, 1985, p. 22.

10   O. Ullrich: *Technik und Herrschaft*, Frankfurt am Main 1977. Also, Weltniveau: *In der Sackgasse des Industriesystems*, Berlin 1979. K. Traube: *Müssen wir umschalten? Von den politischen Grenzen der Technik*, Reinbek 1978, especially ch. 4. L. Mumford: *Mythos der Maschine. Kultur, Technik und Macht*, Frankfurt am Main 1977. J. Naisbitt: *Megatrends*, New York 1982.

11   'Informationalisierung in Japan', *Neues aus Japan* no. 295, November–December 1984, p. 2.

12   M. Jänicke: 'Superindustrialismus und Postindustrialismus' pp. 250ff. 'The employment outlook: where are the jobs in todays's labour market', *OECD Observer* no. 130, September 1984, pp. 5ff. 'Increasing trend toward service jobs', *Economic Impact* no. 2, 1986, pp. 2ff.

13   OECD: *Employment Outlook*, Paris 1985, p. 72.

14   See also H. Kern and M. Schumann: *Das Ende der Arbeitsteilung? Rationalisierung in der industriellen Produktion*. Munich 1985. M.J. Piore and Ch.F. Sabel: *Das Ende der Massenproduktion*, Berlin 1985, J. Naisbitt: Megatrends, ch. 8.

15   For a critique of post-industrialism Cf. P. Gross: *Die Verheissungen der Dienstleistungsgesellschaft. Soziale Befreiung oder Sozialherrrschaft*, Opladen 1983. J. Strasser and K. Traube: *Die Zukunft des Fortschritts*, Berlin and Bonn 1984, pp. 152ff, 238ff. C. Offe: *Arbeitsgesellschaft*, ch. 3. Cf. n. 5 above.

Chapter 9   Tank Syndrome and Bicycle Syndrome

1   M. Jänicke (ed.): *Vor uns die goldenen neunziger Jahre? Langzeitprognosen auf dem Prüfstand*, Munich 1985.

2   N.D. Kondratieff 'Die langen Wellen der Konjunktur', in Parvus et al. *Die langen Wellen, der Konjunktur*, Berlin 1972, originally published in *Archiv für Sozialwissenschaft und Sozialpolitik*, 1926. Cf. *Futures* no. 4, 1981 on this subject; also the literature survey by J. Huber: 'Modell und Theorie der langen Wellen', in M. Jänicke (ed.) *Vor uns die goldenen neunziger Jahre?*

3   G. Mensch: 'Innovation. Ende der Durststrecke', *Wirtschaftswoche* 6 January 1984. J. Huber: *Die verlorene Unschuld der Ökologie*, Frankfurt am Main 1982. Cf. A. Kleinknecht: *Innovation Patterns in Crisis and Prosperity: Schumpeter's Long Cycle Reconsidred*, Enschede 1984.

4   Typically for example, L. Späth: *Wende in die Zukunft*, Reinbek 1985.

5   M. Jänicke; 'Technologische und soziale Innovationen heute', in Senator f. Wissenschaft u. Forschung *Gesellschaftliche Bedingungen technologischer Innovationen*, Berlin 1986, pp. 45ff. F. v. Gottl-Ottlilienfeld: *Wirtschaft und Wissenschaft*, 2 vols. Jena 1931, vol. 1, pp. 294ff, vol. 2, pp. 968ff. Also, *Wirtschaft und Technik*, Tübingen 1923.

6   K. Mannheim: *Mensch und Gesellschaft im Zeitalter des Umbaus*, Bad Homburg, Berlin and Zurich 1967, (originally published in Leiden, 1935).

7   G. Mensch: *Stalemate in Technology: Innovations Overcome the Depression*, Cambridge, Mass. 1979.

8   *Interfutures: Facing the Future*, Paris (OECD) 1979, pp. 127ff, 168, 180, 188. This quotes a paper by Mancur Olson entitled 'The political economy of comparative growth rates'. Cf. M. Olson: *The Rise and Decline of Nations. Economic Growth, Stagflation and Social Rigidities*, New Haven and London 1982. P.F. Whitley: 'The political economy of economic growth', *European Journal of Political Research* 11, 1983, pp. 197ff. L.N. Lindberg and Ch.S. Maier (eds): *The Politics of Inflation and Economic Stagnation. Theoretical Approaches and International Case Studies*, Washington, D.C., 1985.

9   A. King: 'The need for social and institutional innovation', in C.G Hedén and A. King (eds) *Social Innovations for Development*, Oxford 1984, pp. 1ff. Cf. Ch. Freeman: 'Zwischen den Wellen', *Wirtschaftswoche* 8 February 1985, pp. 120ff.

10 M. Jänicke: 'Technologische und soziale Innovationen heute'.

11 T.S. Kuhn: *The Structure of Scientific Revolutions*, Chicago, Ill., 1962, chs 7, 8.

12 K.W. Deutsch: *The Nerves of Government*, Glencoe, Ill. 1963, p. 111.

13 A. Gamble: *Britain in Decline. Economic Policy, Political Strategy and the British State*, London 1985. Whiteley: 'Political economy of economic growth'. Cf. 'Wir sind der arme Mann Europas geworden', *Der Spiegel* No. 11, 1986, pp. 166ff.

14 Cf. for example F.W. Scharpf: 'Die Politik-Verflechtungs-Falle: Europäische Integration und deutscher Föderalismus im Vergleich', *Politische Vierteljahresschrift* 26, no. 4, 1985, pp. 323ff.

15 L.W. Pye: *Aspects of Political Development*, Boston, Mass., 1966, pp. 62ff. Cf. St. Rokkan: 'Die vergleichende Analyse der Staaten-und Nationenbildung: Modelle und Methoden' (originally published in 1967), reprinted in W. Zapf (ed.) *Theorien des sozialen Wandels*, Cologne and Berlin 1969. C.A. Almond and G.B. Powell: *Comparative Politics: A Developmental Approach*, Boston 1966.

16 E.H. Erikson: *Identity: Youth and Crisis*, New York 1968. L. Binder et al.: *Crises and Sequences in Political Development*, Princeton, N.J., 1971. Cf. J. Kohl: Staatsausgaben in Westeuropa, Frankfurt am Main and New York 1984, pp. 157ff.

17 Cf. M. Jänicke: 'Die Analyse des politischen Systems aus der Krisenperspektive', in M. Jänicke (ed.) *Politische Systemkrisen*, Cologne 1973, pp. 19 et pass. E. Altvater: 'Zu einigen Problemen des "Krisenmanagement" in der kapitalistischen Gesellschaft', in M. Jänicke (ed.) *Herrschaft und Krise. Beiträge zur politikwissenschaftlichen Krisenforschung*, Opladen 1973, pp. 170ff.

18 J.M. Buchanan, R.D. Tollison and G. Tullock (eds): *Toward a Theory of the Rent-Seeking Society*, College Station, Tex., 1980. E. Weede: 'Verteilungskoalitionen, Staatstätigkeit und Stagnation', *Politische Vierteljahresschrift* 27, no. 2, 1986.

19 Cf. C.J. Friedrich: *The New Image of the Common Man*, Boston, Mass., 1951.

20 J.A. Schumpeter: Capitalism, Socialism and Democracy, New York 1942, ch. 7.

Chapter 10 State Failure in Scientific Socialism

1 M. Jänicke: 'Umweltpolitik in Osteuropa. Über ungenutzte Möglichkeiten eines Systems', in H. Horn et al. (eds) *Sozialismus in Theorie und Praxis*, Berlin and New York 1978. On this whole subject, J. Füllenbach: *Umweltschutz in Ost und West*, Bonn 1977. U. Weißenburger: 'Umweltprobleme und Umweltschutz in der Sowjetunion', *Berichte des Bundesinstituts für ostwissenschaftliche und internationale Studien* no. 52, 1984, no. 53, 1984, and no. 12, 1985. H. Schreiber: *Umweltprobleme in sozialistischen Ländern. Das Beispiel des oberschlesischen Industriegebietes in der VR Polen*, Wissenschaftszentrum Berlin 1984 (IIUG rep. 84–2). G. Würth: *Umweltschutz und Umweltzerstörung in der DDR*, Frankfurt am Main 1985. W. Gruhn et al.: *Umwelprobleme und Umweltbewußtsein in der DDR*, Cologne 1986. G. Enyedi, A.J. Gijswijt and B. Rhode (eds): *Environmental Policies in East and West*, London 1987. P. Wensierski: Ökologische Probleme und Kritik an der Industriegesellschaft in der DDR heute, Cologne 1988.

2 Th. Weymar: *Im Trabi zu Sonne zur Freiheit. Entwicklung, Folgen und Ursachen des Automobilverkehrs im realen Sozialismus am Beispiel der DDR*, Cologne 1985, pp. 15ff.

3 M. Jänicke: 'Umweltpolitik in China', *Umwelt (VDI)* no. 6, 1975.

4 *Statistisches Jahrbuch für die Bundesrepublik Deutschland* Stuttgart 1989, p. 665.

5 H. Schreiber, 'Umweltprobleme in sozialistischen Ländern'. *3. Immissionsschutzbericht der Bundesregierung 25.4.1984*, Bundestagsdrucksache 10/1354, p. 23. *OECD Environmental Data. Compendium 1985*, Paris (OECD) 1985, p. 19. V. Prittwitz: *Umweltaußenpolitik. Grenzüberschreitende Luftverschmutzung in Europa*, Frankfurt am Main and New York 1984, p. 189.

6 Economic Commission for Europe: *National Strategies and Policies for Air Pollution Abatement*, New York 1987, pp. 40–3.

7 'Waldsterben in der CSSR und in Polen', *Wirtschaft und Umwelt* No. 4, 1984, pp. 12ff. C. Schwartau: 'Die Entwicklung der Umwelt in der DDR', in W. Gruhn et al. *Umweltprobleme und Umweltbewußtsein*. 'Luftverschmutzung in der DDR', *Wirtschaft u. Umwelt* no. la, 1984, pp. 13ff.

8 M. Jänicke, 'Luftverschmutzung: Staub gleichmässig verteilt', *Natur* no. 6, June 1981, p. 95.

9 *DDR-Handbuch*, edited by BM f. innerdeutsche Beziehungen, vol. 2, Cologne 1985, p. 1369.

10 U. Weissenburger: 'Umweltprobleme und Umweltschutz', part I, p. 11.

11 *Statistisches Jahrbuch der DDR 19877*, East Berlin 1987, p. 215. *DIW-Wochenbericht* no. 30/88, p. 380.

12 Writers' collective: Territorialplanung, East Berlin 1976, p. 232.

13 *Statistisches Jahrbuch der DDR*, p. 215. *DIW-Wochenbericht* no. 30/88, p. 380.

14 *Bericht des Generalsekretärs des ZK der KPdSU an den XXVII. Parteitag der Kommunistischen Partei der Sowjetunion, in 27. Parteitag der KPdSU Marz '86:*

Sowjetunion zu neuen Ufern? Dokumente und Materialien mit einer Einleitung v. G. Meyer, Düsseldorf 1986, pp. 23ff.

15 O. Kirchheimer: 'Restriktive Bedingungen und revolutionäre Durchbrüche'. In O. Kirchheimer *Politische Herrschaft*, Frankfurt am Main 1967, pp. 30ff.

16 K. Marx: *Capital*, London 1954, vol. 1, p. 475 (fo. 238).

17 Cf. Ch.K. Chase-Dunn (ed.): *Socialist States in the World System*, Beverly Hills London and New Delhi 1982.

18 Writers' collective, leaders H. Roos & G. Streibel: *Umweltgestaltung und Ökonomie der Naturressourcen*, East Berlin 1979. M.N. Lojter: *Naturressourcen, Umwelt und Investitionseffektivität*, East Berlin originally published in 1977 (in Russian 1974) Cf. ' "Grenzen des Wachstums" im Kommunismus?' *Technologie und Politik* no. 2, Reinbek 1975, pp. 135ff. (Report of a discussion among Soviet scientists).

19 J. Kornai: 'On the present situation and prospects of the Hungarian economy': *Gazdaság* (Budapest) no. 3, 1982, partially reproduced in *Problems of Communism* 33, September–October 1984, p. 13.

20 In W. Sydow (ed.): *In die Zukunft gedacht. Wissenschaftler aus 6 Ländern entwickeln Ideen zu Wissenschaft und Technik*, East Berlin 1983, pp. 140ff.

21 Ibid., p. 153.

22 Ibid., p. 145.

23 'Die Hauptrichtungen der wirtschaftlichen und sozialen Entwicklung der UdSSR für die Jahre 1986 bis 1990 und für den Zeitraum bis zum Jahr 2000 (Planungsdirektive), in: *27. Parteitag der KPdSU*, 379ff.

24 Ibid., pp. 383f.

25 The subject of 'environmental protection' is treated very peripherally in the planning concept of the twenty-seventh party congress. This also applies in a lesser degree to East Germany, which intends to raise lignite production considerably once again, whilst keeping the increase in nuclear energy to a relatively modest 15 per cent. Desulphurization and fluid bed combustion are mentioned in this connection. There is considerable emphasis on the 'material economy'. 'Direktive des XI. Parteitages der SED zum Fünfjahrplan für die Entwicklung der Volkswirtschaft der DDR in den Jahren 1986 bis 1990, *Neues Deutschland* 23 April 1986.

26 M. Jänicke: *Der dritte Weg*, Köln 1964.

Chapter 11 Finale: In Praise of Smaller Units

1 Montesquieu: *The Spirit of the Laws*, London 1909; fo. 252.

2 Cf. G. Geser: 'Kleine Sozialsysteme', *Kölner Zeitschrift für Soziologie und Sozialpsychologie* no. 2, 1980. P. Katzenstein: *Small States in World Markets. Industrial Policy in Europe*, Ithaca, N.Y., 1985.

Methodological Appendix: Political Science as Realistic Analysis

1   Th. Hobbes: *Leviathan.* Everyman's Library, London and New York, p. 16.
2   E. Topitsch: 'Sprachlogische Probleme der sozialwissenschaftlichen Theoriebildung', in E. Topitsch (ed.) *Logik der Sozialwissenschaften,* Cologne and Berlin 1967, pp. 17ff.
3   K. Mannheim: *Ideology and Utopia,* London 1936, repr. 1968, p. 132, fo. 260.
4   Ibid., pp. 129f.
5   J. Habermas: *Legitimationsprobleme im Spätkapitalismus,* Frankfurt am Main 1973, pp. 140ff.
6   St. Hradil: *Die Erforschung der Macht,* Stuttgart 1980, p. 139.
7   M. Jänicke: *Wie das Industriesystem von seinen Mißständen profitiert,* Opladen 1979, p. 16.
8   A. Downs: 'Why Government Budget is too Small in a Democracy', *World Politics* 12 (1960), p. 541.
9   N. Luhmann: 'Zweck-Herrschaft-System. Grundbegriffe und Prämissen Max Webers' in R. Mayntz (ed.) *Bürokratische Organisation,* Cologne and Berlin 1968, p. 41 (originally published 1964).
10 M. Jänicke: *Wie das Industriesystem* pp. 17ff.
11 Cf. P. Massing and P. Reichel (eds): *Interesse und Gesellschaft. Definitionen–Kontroversen–Perspektiven,* Munich 1977.
12 C. Offe: 'Politische Herrschaft und Klassenstrukturen', in G. Kress and D. Senghaas (eds) *Politikwissenschaft,* Frankfurt am Main 1972.
13 J. Tinbergen: 'Do communist and free economies show a converging pattern?' *Soviet Studies* 12, Oxford 1960–1. Z. Brzezinski and S.P. Huntington: *Political Power: USA/USSR,* London 1963, pp. 9ff. Cf. Th. Prager: *Konkurrenz und Konvergenz. Wirtschaft, Umwelt, Wissenschaft,* 1972. A criticism is given by G. Rose: *Konvergenz der Systeme. Legende und Wirklichkeit,* Cologne 1970.
14 See above, chapter 9. G.A. Almond and G.B. Powell: *Comparative Politics. A Developmental Approach,* Boston, Mass., 1966. L. Binder et al.: *Crises and Sequences in Political Development,* Princeton, N.J. 1971.
15 L. Binder et al.: *Crises and Sequences.* Cf. M. Jänicke (ed.): *Herrschaft und Krise,* Opladen, 1973.
16 See above, chapter 9, note 2.

Index

improvement innovation, 127
income privilege (and power), 12
incrementalism, 26
industrial organization, power of,
18–20
industrial power, 15–17, 132
industrial society, 90
see also post-industrialism; superindustrialism
industrial structure, 2
industrial system
bureaucracy–industry complexes,
14–15
definitions, 6–7
functional definitions, 8–10
impotence of parliament, 22–4
nation-state internationalization,
20–2
power of: bureaucracy, 11–13; industrial organization, 18–20; industry,
15–17; media, 17
public interest, 28–30
role of politics, 10–11, 24–8
scapegoat role of politics, 24–8
industrialization (in state socialism),
121–3, 125–6, 129–30
industry
-bureaucracy complexes, 14–15
myth of, 99–101
power of, 15–17
subsidies, 84
inertia, 110, 115, 122, 134
information
dilemmas, 114, 116
quality, 104
services, 101, 103
society, 95
status, 143, 144
Information und Forschung Institut,
45, 88
infrastructure function, 8–9
innovation, 2–3, 52, 56
barriers, 106–11, 126–8
social, 13, 106–7, 107–8, 113–17

stagnation and, 105–6
innovative potential, 99, 102
innovative research, 67
'innovator movements', 114
institutional innovation, 113, 116
'institutional sclerosis', 3, 30, 107,
112, 116
institutionalized deficits, 74–7
instrumentality, 12, 23–4, 25, 140,
141
integration (of socialism into world
market), 124–6
intellectual technology, 94, 106–7, 109
Intellektualtechnik, 106
intensification, 122
interest groups, 23, 26, 108
interest payments (state debt), 74–79
interest positions, 143–4
interests, 15, 16, 23
organizational power of, 20, 21
public, 17–18, 28–30, 118–91, 129,
133, 134
vested, 4, 22, 142, 144
internalization of costs, 32
international agreements, 132–3
international trend, 123–4
internationalization, 7, 20–2
investment, 17

Kahn, Herman, 94, 95
Kiel Institute for World Economy, 82
King, Alexander, 108
Kirchheimer, Otta, 123
Kirsch, Guy, 71
Kondratieff cycles, 106, 108
Kornai, Janos, 127
Kruschev, N., 119

labour market policies, 85
laissez-faire policies, 3, 66, 68, 77, 100,
112, 114
Land Berlin (West), 60
Land Culture Law (1979), 119
land protection, 46

INDEX 169

quantitative indicators, 70, 71
quantity (of public goods), 36–7

railway industry, 81, 83, 84
rationalization, 7, 11, 70, 103
raw materials, 95, 98–9, 101, 102, 125, 129–30
Reagan administration, 82
realist world view, 138, 139–40
realistic analysis (political science as), 135–41
realistic post-industrialism, 104
Realtechnik, 106
Recktenwald, H.C., 31, 33, 34–5
regional structures, 96
regulatory function, 8
Reich, Robert B., 65
reindustrialization, 103
rent-seeking society, 113
repair stage (environment), 51
resources, 98–9, 129–30
    structural policy, 65–73
    see also raw materials
rigidity see tank syndrome
risk, 98, 116
road freight, 81, 83, 120–1
road traffic complex, 15
road transport, 55–59, 81, 83–4, 120–1
routinization, 11
Russian revolution (1917), 123
RWE, 60, 79

saturation trend (innovation), 127
Scharpf, Fritz, 66
Schmitt, Carl, 4
scientific complex, 15
scientific revolution, 122
scientific socialism
    advantages, 118–19
    barriers to innovation, 126–8
    conclusion (are politics impotent), 128–30

disadvantages, 120–3
integration, 124–6
international trend, 123–4
security complex, 15
security issues, 15, 22, 37
Seebohm (Transport Minister), 57
self-employment, 86
self-help, 28, 72
self-realization, 102, 103, 126
services sector, 7, 71, 95, 99–104
Small Business Administration (US), 103
small units, 131–4
smokestack industries, 50, 53, 65, 70, 71, 103
social–industrial complex, 36, 37, 79
social change, 137–8, 146
social costs, 6, 112
    of world market, 89–92, 100–1, 115
Social Democratic Party, 53, 62
social engineering, 106–7, 108–9, 114
'social industries', 97
social innovations, 13, 106–7, 107–8, 113–17
social power, 10
'social rigidities', 108
social sciences (world views), 138–41
social security, 13, 34, 41–2, 108
social structure, 108, 110, 125, 130
socialism, 6
sovereignty, 20, 21, 91
Soviet planning, 129–30
Sozialtechnik, 106
specialization, 7, 8, 11, 14, 38, 97
speed limits, 56–7, 58
stagnation, 2, 105–6
Stalin, Joseph, 121, 125
standards, 137–8, 139
state
    activity (as production), 33–4
    functional definition, 8–10
    indebtedness see debt (state indebtedness)
    machinery see machinery of state

Index by Jackie McDermott